USING MOTHER TONGUES IN THE LEARNING/TEACHING OF ENGLISH AS A FOREIGN LANGUAGE: A CASE STUDY

WAKENGE MALEKANI CLAUDE

Copyright © 2025 WAKENGE MALEKANI CLAUDE

No part of this book may be reproduced, distributed, or transmitted in any form or by any means, including photocopying, recording, or other electronic or mechanical methods, without the prior written permission of the publisher and the author, except in the case of brief quotations used in reviews or certain other noncommercial uses permitted by copyright law.

Publisher: Upway Books
Author: WAKENGE MALEKANI CLAUDE
Title: USING MOTHER TONGUES IN THE LEARNING/TEACHING OF ENGLISH AS A FOREIGN LANGUAGE: A CASE STUDY
ISBN: 978-1-917916-85-1
Cover Designed on Canva: www.canva.com

This book is a work of non-fiction. The information it contains is based on the author's research, experience, and knowledge at the time of publication. The publisher and authors have made every effort to ensure the accuracy and reliability of the information provided, but assume no responsibility for any errors, omissions, or differing interpretations of the subject matter. This publication is not intended to replace professional advice or consultation. Readers are encouraged to seek professional guidance where appropriate.

contact@upwaybooks.com
www.upwaybooks.com

DEDICATION

I dedicate this dissertation to:

- My parents Wakenge Vumilia and Malekani Kapele.
- My wife Louange Eda.
- My children Levidi and Claudia.

ACKNOWLEDGEMENTS

I thank the Almighty God for His love and mercy, granting me physical, moral and spiritual strength, protection and abilities to carry out this dissertation.

I express my sincere gratitude to my supervisor, Professor Nsimambote Zola, who kindly agreed to supervise this dissertation.

I would like to thank my co-supervisor, Professor Buhendwa Munganga, for his contribution to this dissertation.

I would like to thank a member of my reading committee Professor Busaki, for guiding and assisting me with his valuable insight in this dissertation.

I am grateful to Professor Majambo Kalonda for his initial supervision.

I also thank Mr. Kalala for accepting to teach the first year students of media in using a multilingual approach or translanguaging method on my behalf.

I thank my siblings: Vianney Malekani, Olga, David, Lydie.

I thank those in the family of Christ for their continual moral and spiritual support, especially Professor Mundeke and his wife.

I want to thank all the lecturing staff of the University of Kinshasa and particularly the Association of scientific staff of the University of Kinshasa (ACS) for their last-minute financial support.

I cannot forget the first-year students of 'LMD' in the Department of Media and Information, Faculty of Arts, who willingly agreed to fill out the questionnaires and be involved in the interview for data collection.

I wish to express my sincere gratitude to the authorities of the language observatory for providing me with the opportunity to work there, which helps me fund partially my own research and for their scientific contribution.

This dissertation would also not have been completed without the efforts of the following people to whom I would like to express my deepest gratefulness: Etienne Ngwaba, Martin Dunia, Gaby kyomba and his wife, Degbalase Ngbendu Celestin, Atuba Pascal, René Mayamba and Matondo who are all my support in Statistics involved in this dissertation.

LIST OF ABBREVIATIONS AND ACRONYMS

ACALAN	: African academy of languages
A F D L	: Alliance des Forces Démocratiques pour la Libération du Congo.
A L	: Applied Linguistics
C A	: Contrastive Analysis
CAR	: Central African Republic.
CELTA	: Centre de Linguistique Théorique et Appliqué.
C L I L	: Content and language integrated learning
CTL	: Communicative Teaching Language
DRC	: Democratic Republic of Congo
E A	: Error Analysis
EAL	: English as additional language.
EFL	: English as a foreign language
EIC	: Etat Independent du Congo.
GCSE	: General certificate of secondary Education
GTM	: Grammar Translation Method
IBM	: International Business Machines
IL	: Interlanguage
L1	: First Language
L2	: Second Language
LMD	: Licence Master Doctorat
MPR	: Mouvement Populaire de la Révolution
MT	: Mother Tongue
NL	: Native Language
SPSS	: Statistical Package for Social Sciences
TL	: Target language
TPR	: Total Physical Response
U N C	: Université Nationale du Congo
UNESCO	: United Nations Educational, Scientific and Cultural Organization.

TABLE OF CONTENTS

DEDICATION 3
ACKNOWLEDGEMENTS 4
LIST OF ABBREVIATIONS AND ACRONYMS iv
TABLE OF CONTENTS 6
  INTRODUCTION 10
CHAPTER ONE: REVIEW OF THE LITERATURE 14
I.1.   Definitions of some key concepts. 14
I.1.1.   Terms related to languages 14
I.1.1.1. The Mother Tongue (MT) 14
I.1.1.   3. Multilingual education 17
I.1.1.   4. Mother-tongue education 17
I.1.1.5. Intercultural education: 18
I.1.1.6. Second language (L2) 18
I.1.1.7. Vernacular language 19
I.1.1.8. National language 19
I.1.1.9. Official language 20
I.1.1.10. Lingua franca 20
I.1.1.   11. Foreign language (FL) 21
I.1.1.12. Language of instruction 21
I.1.1.13. Language of choice 21
I.1.1.14. Inter African languages 22
I.1.1.15. Perfect mother tongue 22
I.1.2.   Terms 23
I.1.3.   Related to culture 23
I.1.2.2. Acculturation 23
I.1.2.3. Cultural integration 23
I.1.4.   Terms related to teaching I.1.3.1.Teaching 23
I.1.5.   Terms related to learning 24
I.1.4.2. Learner: 24

I.2. The Sociolinguistic Situation of the Democratic Republic of Congo 24
I.2.1. Languages spoken in the DRC 24
I.2.2. Language policy in the DRC before and after independence.. 26
I.2.2.2. Independent State of Congo (1885-1908) 27
I.2.2.3. Belgian Congo (1908-1960) 28
I.2.2.4. Post-colonial period 29
I.2.2.5. Studies on Mother tongues in the DRC 38
I.3. Previous works on Mother tongues and the use of mother tongue in EFL classrooms 45
I.3.1. Previous works on Mother tongues 45
I.5.2. Previous works on the use of Mother tongues in EFL classrooms. 56

CHAPTER TWO: METHODOLOGY 66
II.1. Population and sampling methods 66
II.1.2. Sampling methods 67
II.2. Data sources 69
II.4.4. Methods used in data interpretation 77
III.1 Coding 108
III.2 Survey data analysis 111
III.2.1 Survey data identification variables 111
III.2.1.1 Gender 111
III.2.1.2 Age 112
III.2.2 Survey data research interest variables 113
III.2.2.2 Languages used in a quarrel 115
III.2.2.3 Languages of smooth expression 115
III.2.2.4 Languages used in trouble 117
Figure 6. languages used in trouble 117
III.2.2.5 Languages of intimacy expression 117
Figure 7: languages of intimacy expression 118
III.2.2.6 Languages of mass media 118

III.2.2.7 Languages of confided in writing 119

III.2.2.7 Languages of confided in reading 120

III.2.2.8 Languages of easy understanding 121

III.2.2.9 Languages preferred to follow classes 122

   III.2.2.10 Languages preferred to follow sermons in church 123

III.2.2.11 Languages preferred to follow english classes 124

III.2.2.12 Views of the respondents concerning multilingualism in teaching English 126

III. 3 Interview data analysis 128

III.3.1 Interview data identification variables 128

III.3.1.1 Gender 128

III.3.1.2 Age 129

III.3 .2 Interview data research interest variables 129

   III.3.2.2 Languages used in a quarrel 130

III.3.2.3 Languages of smooth expression 130

   III.3.2.4. Languages expressed in trouble 131

III.3.2.5. Languages of intimacy expression 131

III.3.2.6. Languages of mass media 132

III.3.2.7. Languages confided in writing 132

III.3.2.8. Languages confided in reading 133

III.3.2.9. Languages of easy understanding 134

   III.3.2.10. Languages of preference to follow classes 134

III.3.2.11. Languages of preference to attend religious sermons in church 135

III.3.2.12. Languages of preference to follow english classes 135

III.3.2.13. Views of the participants concerning mutilingualism in teaching english 136

III.4 The results of the monolingual and multilingual teaching tests. 139

III.4.1 Monolingual teaching test results 139

III.4.2 Multilingual teaching test results 141

III. 5. Interpretation 143
III. 5.1 Gender 143
III.5.2 Age 145
III.5.3 Languages expressed in a court 146
III.5.4 Languages used in a quarrel 147
III. .5. 5 Languages of smooth expression 148
III. .5. 6. Languages used in trouble 149
III. .5. 7 Languages of intimacy 150
III. .5. 8 Languages of mass media 151
III.5.9 Languages confided in writing 151
III. .5. 10 Languages confided in reading 152
III.5. 12 Languages of preference to follow classes 154
III.5. 13 Languages of preference to follow sermon in church 155
III.5.14 Languages of preference to follow English classes 156
III.5.15 Views of the participants concerning multilingualism in teaching triangulated 157
III. 6. FINDINGS 159
III. 6 .1 Identifying the participants' perfect mother tongues 159
CHAPTER FOUR: RECOMMENDATIONS 163
IV.1. Approaches in EFL 163
IV.2. Some recommendations 174
CONCLUSION 177
RECOMMENDATIONS 183
Recommendations to the Ministry of Education 183
Recommendations to EFL teachers 184
BIBLIOGRAPHY 185
APPENDICES 220

INTRODUCTION

01. The research problem

The benefits of integrating mother tongues in teaching a foreign language are sufficiently documented in the literature of multilingualism and education according to Hinai (2011), Mahmutoglu and Kicir (2013) and Richards (2016). The latter states that integrating mother tongues in teaching English as a foreign language helps learners understand and remember new words.

Taking into account the above fact concerning the positive impact of mother tongues in the teaching of English as a foreign language, the researcher is interested in conducting a study to demonstrate this positive impact in a classroom.

02. Interest of the topic

This dissertation is an innovative study. It deals with a multilingual approach which can help Congolese students and teachers in the teaching and learning of English as a foreign language. Many scholars have demonstrated benefits of multilingual approach helping in explaining the meaning of abstract words, highlighting the main differentes in grammar and pronunciation between L1 and L2.

03. Research objectives

This dissertation aims at demonstrating the positive impact of mother tongue in the teaching of English as a foreign language.

It targets the following three objectives:

- To establish the perfect mother tongue of the participants.
- To find out the impact between learners taught in mono and multilingual

teaching
- To suggest the multilingual approach in teaching English in order to help out in EFL classrooms.

04. Research questions

For Kothari (2004), research questions clearly reflect the research topic. They also determine the scope of a study. The three research questions below are used in this dissertation.

- What is the perfect mother tongue of participants?
- Is there an impact between monolingual teaching and multilingual one?
- Is multilingual teaching approach appropriate for participants?

05. Hypotheses

Ahuja (2001) defines a hypothesis as an assumption about relationships between variables and a tentative explanation of the research problem or a guess about the research outcome.

The following research outcomes expected are:

- Most of participants have Lingala and French as perfect mother tongues.
- There is a positive impact between learners taught in monolingual teaching and those taught in multilingual one, which is demonstrated statistically.
- The multilingual teaching approach, which shows a positive impact, is appropriate for participants.

06. Research design

Research design is defined by Leedy (1997) as a plan for a study providing the overall framework for data.

For this study, the researcher used double sequential explanatory models of mixed methods design that includes both quantitative study (survey questionnaire) and qualitative study (interview) and quantitative (tests). The data were collected from a sample of students. Those students were randomly selected. Double sequential mixed methods are used because they complement each other to answer all research questions effectively. (Durkheim, 2004).

07. Field of the study

This dissertation falls in the broad field of applied linguistics including social aspects of language use, that is sociolinguistics, and aspects of language teaching, that is applied linguistics strictly speaking. It covers both sociolinguistics and teaching-learning aspects of language. In other words, in this dissertation, sociolinguistics solves a problem related to the language use and applied linguistics related to the teaching and learning of English language.

08. Theoretical framework

This dissertation examines an interdisciplinary topic s and is based on three main theories: translanguaging, multilingual theory, and classical test theory. Translanguaging is a theory that explains how people use different languages in everyday life. It involves using multiple languages while teaching. (García, O., & Wei, L. (2014). It involves the simultaneous use of two languages while teaching (Cen Williams, 1980).

Multilingual theory focuses on the existence of various languages in a specific geographic area. Individuals in such areas may speak only one language or multiple languages. (Otwinowska-Kaztelanic, A, 2011). Classical test theory is commonly used to assess grammar skills. (Novick, 1966).

It is a traditional method for evaluating the reliability and validity of a test based on its items. This theory is also known as the true score model. (Cappeleri, 2014).

09. Delimitation of the work

This study is restricted to a specific time and place as follows:

It is carried out in the period going from 2021 to 2024 at the University of Kinshasa, the Faculty of Arts, mainly in the department of media. This choice is justified by the proximity and availability of necessary data collection.

10. The work outline

Apart from the introduction and conclusion, the current dissertation is divided into four chapters as follows: the introduction includes key concepts definitions; the first chapter is about the review of literature. The second one describes the research design and methodology. The third one is the results (interpretation). The fourth one focuses on discussion and the last one concerns some recommendations.

CHAPTER ONE: REVIEW OF THE LITERATURE

This chapter contains four sections. The first section deals with definitions of some key concepts. The second and third ones concern respectively the sociolinguistic situation of the DRC and studies on the mother tongue in the DRC. The fourth and the last one provide the previous works on the use of mother tongues in EFL classrooms.

I.1. Definitions of some key concepts.

I.1.1. Terms related to languages

Twenty two key concepts that are worth defining are: the Mother Tongue, second language, vernacular language, the national language, the foreign language, the lingua franca and other related concepts.

I.1.1.1. The Mother Tongue (MT)

For the concept 'Mother Tongue', seven definitions have been retained, starting from UNESCO's.

According to UNESCO (1953), "mother tongue" (MT), also known as first language (L1) or Native language (NL) or home language: ''is the language or languages that a person has learned since birth and/or is most familiar with.

It is important to note that a person's language does not have to be his mother tongue, as everyone has his own unique language background.

This language is used for thinking, dreaming, and counting. It is a language that a person has become proficient in and is the primary one they use.

The terms mother tongues, first languages, or native languages are all used to describe the language(s) that a person has known since birth or is most comfortable with. These terms are used because each person has his own language history.

UNESCO's definition obviously includes two elements, a chronological one and a competence one. While the first is pretty natural and a straightforward one, as is the case for MTs in monolingual countries, the second element is more difficult to define, particularly in multilingual countries.

It is, for example, easy to define and consider French as the general MT of French men; it is not the case for defining the MT(s) of Congolese people, even of Bakongo, Baluba, Baswahili and Bangala people! UNESCO and other organizations have identified the first criterion as achievable, but the second criterion always leads to discussions about which language a multilingual speaker uses most often.

According to UNESCO (2003), the most effective way to teach a child is in their mother tongue. This is because their mind naturally processes information through familiar signs, making it easier for them to express themselves and understand concepts. Additionally, speaking their mother tongue helps a child feel connected and recognized within their community. Learning in their mother tongue also allows a child to acquire knowledge faster compared to learning in a foreign language. For example, they can grasp a subject much more quickly when it is taught in their own language.

Online dictionaries define "mother tongue" or "first language" (L1) as the language a person learns from birth. It is also referred to as a dominant language, home language, or native language. Before, people used to call their mother tongue their homeland language

According to UNESCO (2017), this is the main language that is spoken regularly from birth at home and usually used as the first language from parents.

It is the 'first language' or languages that the child learns at an early age in an environment where the language is spoken. However, a child may have several first languages, for example by having parents who speak two or more languages. In the 60's mother tongue was called homeland language" to refer to the ancestral language spoken at home. (Hernandez, 2018)

Wahdaniyah J. (2017) points that a child may have different mother tongues only if those languages are spoken equally often so that the child learns them at the same time.

According to the Oxford Advanced Learner's Dictionary (2007), a mother tongue is the language that you first learn to speak when you are a child. According to Cobuild Advanced Learner's Dictionary (1987) and Cambridge Advanced Learner's Dictionary (1995), it is the language that you learn from your parents when you are a baby.

If a person no longer understands the first language he or she learned, the second language is the one they learned. For someone who learned two languages simultaneously in early childhood, "mother tongue" is the most commonly spoken language at home before going to school.

A person may only have two mother tongues if the two languages are used at the same time and are understood by the same person. In conclusion, a mother tongue is the first language, native language, home language or dominant language of a multilingual person. These different terms are used alternatively.

I.1.1.2 Multilingualism

Multilingualism is defined as the use of three or more languages; It is the ability to communicate in multiple languages (Larissa Aronin, 2018). Generally, multilingualism refers to the coexistence of multiple languages within a country, community. Neuroscientists delve into the topic of multilingualism by examining how the brain is structured in individuals who are proficient in more than one language.

I.1.1. 3. Multilingual education

A Multilingual education refers to the use of more languages as a medium of instruction. The term "multilingual education" refers to the use of at least three languages—the mother tongue, a regional or national language, and an international language in education (UNESCO, 2003).

Furthermore, UNESCO urges an adequate supply of reading material in mother tongues to learners "for entertainment, as well, as for study'. It is an approach that involves using two or more languages as the medium of instruction. In other words; it implies the formal use of multiple languages in the curriculum.

In countries where there are multiple regional languages or more than one official language that include both the mother tongues of children and the widely spoken languages of the nation. (UNESCO, 2003)

I.1.1. 4. Mother-tongue education

Mother-tongue education refers to the use of a person's native language as the main language of instruction (UNESCO, 2015). Teaching involves an instructor, a goal, and a context made up of elements that can be controlled by the instructor (such as teaching methods) and those that cannot (like class size and school facilities) (Smith, 1963).

Teaching is a dynamic process that primarily involves conversations between teachers and students during specific activities (Edmund, 1967).

It follows a scientific approach with key components including content, communication, and feedback (Gagne et al, 1974).

I.1.1.5. Intercultural education:

Intercultural education involves teaching people to appreciate and understand different cultures, helping them adapt and thrive in a community that respects these differences.

It emphasizes the importance of building relationships with individuals from diverse backgrounds, including those with different languages, religions, cultures, and perspectives.

This kind of education is important for dealing with differences in gender, social class, and economic status, along with cultural differences like beliefs, values, and traditions. By appreciating and accepting diversity, intercultural education can improve the social, cultural, and economic health of a community or setting. (Chiriac, Argentina, 2013)

I.1.1.6. Second language (L2)

According to UNESCO (2015), a second language (L2) is a language that a person learns in addition to their native language. It is often called the official language, especially in countries that have been colonised.

A second language is typically a language that is necessary for education, work, and daily activities, as mentioned by Saville-Troike (2006).

A Second language acquisition occurs when someone learns a new language in a place where it is not the native language, as noted by Henrici & Vollmer (2001).

When a person learns a second language, they start with the language he or She learned as a child, which is typically the one spoken by their family. (Gass and Selinker, 2008).

Learning a second language involves intentionally learning a new language that is not the same as their first one.

I.1.1.7. Vernacular language

Is a native, local language spoken either by a rural or urban speech community or by a lower social class, it is informal or usual the least standardized (Li Ming, 2020)

I.1.1.8. National language

Holmes (2001) defines it as the language of a political, cultural, and social group, and it is often created and used to represent national unity. A national language is a language or its variant, like a dialect, that is linked to a group of people and the area they live in. Generally, national languages are the languages spoken in a specific region, often a nation-state, by one or more groups. This connection means that a national language is tied to a place, but it can also serve as a way for different groups within a nation to communicate. Ultimately, a national language represents a community of speakers, which may not always align with a formal state, but it is important for communication and identity. (Fathi, 2023).

National language is the language of political, social and cultural entity and national integration (UNESCO, 1953). According to the constitution, the Democratic Republic of Congo recognizes four national languages: Ciluba, Kikongo, Lingala, and Kiswahili.

I.1.1.9. Official language

According to Holmes (op. cit), an official language is a language used for government business in some areas like the court, parliament, and administration. It may not be widely spoken in society, but sometimes one language can serve as both the national and official language. Official Language is the language used by government institutions, including courts, legislatures, and administrative bodies. It is also the language used in schools for teaching and learning at all levels. Often, the constitution specifically states which language is the Official Language, along with any other National Languages that may exist. (Fathi, op cit).

The difference is that national language is used for political, cultural, and social functions, whereas the official language is used for government business such as the national court, parliament, and business.

I.1.1.10. Lingua franca.

Matthews (2007) defined Lingua franca as any language used for communication between groups who have no other language in common. The term goes back to a variety of Vulgar Latin spoken in the South of Italy, mainly for trade (UNESCO, 1953).

Ciluba, Kikongo, Kiswahili, and Lingala are good examples of lingua franca in the DRC. They are all used for wider and intertribal communication in the eastern, northern, central and western parts of the Democratic Republic of Congo.

I.1.1. 11. Foreign language (FL)

A Foreign language (FL), is 'a language that is taught as a school subject but which is neither used as a medium of instruction in school nor as a language of communication within a country' (Gumperz, 2010). English is a foreign language in the DRC. Let us note that in many countries, particularly developed one, foreign languages are optional as school subjects, for example, French in England or English in France or Germany. The status of English in the DRC is clearly not the same as in these countries. It may be regarded as a midpoint between an official (second) language and a foreign language (Malekani, 2006).

For instance, in the DRC, English is a foreign language and its use is mandatory from secondary to post-secondary schools. Recently, a Ministerial Decree has made it a "transversal" at all levels of higher education and universities. It is not spoken at all in any national Congolese community, despite its growing use in some areas.

I.1.1.12. Language of instruction

The language used for teaching the basic curriculum or core subjects in the educational system is referred to as school language inside or outside the classroom (UNESCO, 2003).

I.1.1.13. Language of choice

Language choice is a sociolinguistic concept that involves selecting languages for specific purposes in different situations. The decision to use a particular language can be conscious or unconscious, but it always occurs within a specific context, such as a speech community. Language choices are important in communication, as noted by Holmes (2013).

This means that when people communicate, they often select a specific language. In multilingual communities, individuals may use more than two languages. When speakers use multiple languages, it shows they are making a language choice. They might choose one language or mix languages while interacting. People select the right language for their conversation, switch languages, and use different languages depending on the situation.

I.1.1.14. Inter African languages

Inter-African languages like Kiswahili in East Africa and Lingala in the Democratic Republic of Congo and Congo Brazzaville are commonly used for communication between countries.

These languages were officially recognized and discussed in the most recent report from the Conference on Language Policies in Zimbabwe in 1997.

They are important for education and business.

I.1.1.15. Perfect mother tongue

Woolston (2015) defined perfect mother tongue by mentioning the following three criteria: firstly, it is a language learned from childhood; secondly it is spoken competently by the speaker basing on the four language skills. Lastly, the speaker sounds native like when speaking it.

Li (2008) defined perfect mother tongue as a true language of an expert in multiple languages. Nsimambote (2024) defined perfect mother tongue as the easier and emotional language of a multilingual person after establishing sociopsycholinguistic parameters. In conclusion, a perfect mother tongue is any language used daily with a high proficiency.

I.1.2. Terms

I.1.3. Related to culture

I.1.2.1. Enculturation

For Stephen A. and Marvin K. (1988), it can be defined as a process of learning one's own culture.

I.1.2.2. Acculturation

Which is a process of learning another culture. (Stephen and Marvin, op cit)

I.1.2.3. Cultural integration

One of the scholars who studied this topic is Durkheim (1951). He believed that cultural integration is a process that allows individuals or groups within a social system to connect with each other in a meaningful way. Essentially, cultural integration involves the evolution of behaviors, attitudes, everyday habits, beliefs, and more (Wanner et al., 2002)

I.1.4. Terms related to teaching I.1.3.1.Teaching

Edmund (2019) teaching as "an interactive process that mainly consists of dialogue occurring in the classroom between the teacher and the student, taking place during specific identifiable activities.

I.1.3.2. the teacher plays a significant role in finding new ways for students to learn (Zamroni, 2001).

I.1.5. Terms related to learning

I.1.4.1. Learning

Learning is a person's effort to achieve an overall new change in behavior as a result of their experience of interacting with their environment (Slameto, 1995). In addition, learning is a process by which human beings acquire a vast variety of competencies, skills, and attitudes (Wahyuni, 2010).

I.1.4.2. Learner:

Learner is a person who learns, according to the online Collins dictionary, or is someone who is learning about a particular subject or how to do something.

I.2. The Sociolinguistic Situation of the Democratic Republic of Congo

In this section, the researcher presents the situation of the language during the colonial period and what prevails today, as some authors have had to point out, as well as, Congolese and foreigners in general (Africans, Westerners, etc.).

I.2.1. Languages spoken in the DRC

The Democratic Republic of Congo is a multilingual country with approximately 450 different ethnic groups, where nearly 242 languages are spoken.

Among these, Ciluba, Kikongo, Kiswahili, and Lingala have been recognized as national languages, while French serves as the official language. While French is commonly spoken as a second or third language by most Congolese. Studies indicate that only a minority use it as their first language. In

Kinshasa, the capital city, the majority of the population speak French and Lingala. Various statistics suggest that there are 7 million Kasai speakers, 11.1 million speakers of Congolese Kiswahili in the Eastern regions, and 5 million Kikongo speakers.

Ndolo (1992) presented the situation of national languages with the percentage of their speakers as follows:

Table 1: number of speakers in different geographical areas

Language	Number of speakers	Area
Ciluba	19.30 %	Kasaï, Bandundu
Kikongo	15.75%	Bas-Congo, Bandundu
Kiswahili	27.49 %	Katanga, Kivu (Maniema, Sud Kivu, Nord Kivu) South East of the province Orientale (Kisangani, Bunia)
Lingala	37.46 %	Kinshasa, Equateur, Bandundu, Province orientale

As for Kamwangamalu (1996), he has represented these national languages in the table with the respective geographical areas where they are spoken as follows:

Table 2: Geographical areas where these national languages are used

N°	Language	Geographical area	Speakers (%)
01	Ciluba	Eastern Kasai province, Western Kasai province Katanga	10
02	Kikongo	Bandundu, Lower Zaire Province	12
03	Kiswahili	Katanga, Upper Zaire province Kivu, province (North-Kivu, South –Kivu and Maniema.)	23
04	Lingala	Kinshasa District, Equateur, Province Upper Zaire Province.	14

According to Ntawakuderwa (1986) Lingala should be recognised as an independent national language while Kamwangamalu (1997) has shown support for Kiswahili.

I.2.2. Language policy in the DRC before and after independence.
I.2.2.1. In Pre-Colonial Period

Prior to the establishment of the EIC, the Democratic Republic of Congo had various kingdoms and empires. Notable among them were Kongo, Luba, and Kuba. Additionally, the empire of Lunda held prominence in the region. It is believed that the empire of Lunda primarily used one language for communication, while the kingdoms, such as Kongo, used another language.

The question arises as to which languages were used for internal and external communication within these entities. Were the inhabitants of these kingdoms and empires compelled to learn these languages through educational institutions or military training? Conversely, some argue that distinct populations were dispersed throughout the nation. Considering the fact that these entities were either multilingual empires or monolingual kingdoms, it appears that significant communication barriers were not prevalent.

Furthermore, there existed a connection between Portugal and the Kingdom of Kongo. However, it remains unclear which language the Kingdom of Kongo used in written communication and the level of difficulty they encountered when interacting with the Portuguese.

I.2.2.2. Independent State of Congo (1885-1908)

In the early stages of Belgian dominance over Congo the challenge of incorporating local languages into education posed a significant obstacle for the colonizers. To deal with the linguistic complexities of the newly independent state various solutions were proposed through a series of decisions and legal actions.

These included Circular No. 6 of 1967 which banned the use of French in official interactions with Congolese natives and soldiers as well as Circular No. 41 of July 1 1895 which stressed the need for European Community officials to develop vocabulary in the different indigenous dialects. In addition Circular No. 62 was implemented to establish regulations for the spelling of geographic names in Congo. Furthermore an agreement was signed on May 26, 1906 advocating for the use of Belgian national languages instead of studying Congolese languages. This agreement was accompanied by the establishment of agricultural and vocational schools on May 4 1902 a mere two years after the formation of Congo as an independent State.

After achieving independence French was declared as the official language for the State government and judiciary while missionary efforts were carried out in mother tongues.

The first instance of the French language being introduced was in 1902 when school colonies were founded for orphaned and abandoned children.

I.2.2.3. Belgian Congo (1908-1960)

The Charter of Colonization was introduced by the Belgian Congo government on 18 October 1908. Although it did not specifically address the languages spoken in the country, it emphasized the importance of both Flemish and French, the languages spoken in Belgium.

Many significant laws were written and distributed in both Flemish and French. Following meetings in Stanleyville, Kisangani, and Kisantu in 1910, missionaries decided to begin teaching children in their native languages at the elementary level. This initiative prompted the colonizers to consider standardising the various languages spoken in the region.

They aimed to document key versions of these languages and promote a common language for the country through specific measures. In May 1912, Colonial Circular No.68 was issued, highlighting the significance of teaching in local languages and indicating a desire among the people of Belgium to adapt to the country's circumstances.

The Colonial Congress of 1920 and the Franck Commission of 1922 focused on strategies for teaching the national language in schools.

Discussions between the government and religious groups resurfaced language issues once again.

According to Article 3 of the agreements, the colonial government compensated 3,000 francs for each native language documented by the missions, which included a grammar book, vocabulary list, and a map indicating the regions where the language was spoken.

I.2.2.4. Post-colonial period

Regarding language policy in the Democratic Republic of Congo, it has undergone significant changes since independence. Initially, there was confusion surrounding the use of local languages in daily life. However, important decisions were made to address this issue.

For example, Decree No.174, issued on October 17, 1962, focused on restructuring the primary education system, leading to the phasing out of local languages in schools. One major outcome of this decree was the establishment of a single national language for all official purposes.

In 1968, the Education Reform Commission held its first session, where it recommended the introduction of bilingualism (French and local languages) in primary schools.

Subsequently, during the second session of the commission, there was a proposal to incorporate regional languages into the primary education curriculum.

A. Communiqué No. 253/0158/25/68 of 1968 (Ministry of Culture and Tourism) Decided to promote and disseminate four national languages, but did not specify how the decision would be implemented.
B. The first regular congress of the MPR (1972) called for the study and teaching of Zairian languages at all levels, but there was no follow-up.

In 1974, the Lubumbashi Linguistic Seminar made a request for national languages to be reintroduced in primary schools. However, there was no follow- up on this matter.

Moving forward to 1982, the Third Ordinary Congress of the MPR decided that there would be no specific guidelines regarding the use of national languages. Then, in 1992 and 1993, the country's sovereign national conference of active forces called for the four indigenous languages, along with French, to be recognized as official languages. Unfortunately, this idea remains a mere fantasy and will never be put into action.

The land holds great cultural significance and is protected and promoted by the state. Since the colonial era, four indigenous languages, namely Kikongo, Tshiluba, Lingala, and Kiswahili, have been officially used as national languages.

Lingala is the only African language that President Mobutu predominantly used in public settings.

However, the promotion of Sango, a language used for commercial purposes on the northern border with the Central African Republic, was not successful due to the dominance of Lingala. Lingala is the most widely spoken of the four national languages and has been the primary language since independence, especially in the capital city.

In urban areas with a high number of multi-ethnic marriages, Lingala is the language spoken by the majority of children. It is also the language used by children in Swahili-speaking regions. A map at the end of this document provides a summary of the distribution of major languages, although it is not comprehensive enough to determine the languages spoken in specific areas. Barbara Yates (1980) states that a Zairian person may speak their mother tongue at home or with other members of their ethnic group, French at work, or Lingala as a regional commercial language during market conversations. More broadly, President Mobutu frequently spoke to audiences speaking Kiswahili in the city of Bukavu and other locations by using Lingala in his speeches. His argument that Kiswahili was unacceptable in Zaire was politicized by doing this and was connected to the existence of Arab slave traders.

Concerning the sociolinguistic pyramid, four levels can be mentioned:

Level 1: we have almost 250 ethnic languages.

Level 2: we have four national languages. These languages are Ciluba (a local language), Kikongo (a local language), Kiswahili (a local language), and Lingala (a local language).

In the DRC, Kikongo is spoken in two provinces – Kongo Central and Bandundu but it is also spoken with particular accents in other countries like Gabon, Congo Brazza ville and Angola. Lingala is also used in the province of Kinshasa and the five present provinces of former Equateur as well as in two of the former 'province orientale'. It is generally used in each province as lingua franca.

Kiswahili: spoken throughout most of the Eastern part of the Democratic Republic of Congo now in nine provinces: North Kivu, South Kivu, Maniema, Katanga, two former provinces of Kasai, Kinshasa, and former Province Orientale etc.).

It is also used in primary schools, and partly in the national and international press (some BBC and German TV programs are in Swahili), evangelization, etc. Outside our borders, the language is spoken in Tanzania, Uganda, Zambia and Kenya.

Ciluba: is a Bantu language spoken exclusively in the Democratic Republic of Congo, specifically in the two former provinces of Kasai Oriental and Occidental; It is a language of education, oral and written press, courts, administration and evangelization in this region of Kasai. Note that Ciluba comes in two variants: Luba and Lulwa (Mubiayi Mamba, 2015).

Level 3: the official language: French. According to the language policy introduced in 1963, it is that of the 1954 reform, which officially made French the only language of instruction (see decree Art. 3 of October 17, 1962).

Level 4: English taught as a foreign language. Let us mention that French is the high language (H) which means it is on top and the national languages are the low language (L) which means it is at the bottom. The fact that H is valued more highly than L and has more specialized roles and uses in the community is one of the characteristics of diaglossia, according to Ferguson (1954).

French is still widely spoken today, although some researchers claim that only a small proportion of Congolese can speak or write it (e.g. Rubengo: only 30% can get it right).

Calvet (1993) defined language planning as the "passage à l'acte," or the actual application of a language policy. The deliberate choices made about how a language or languages interact with social life are referred to as language policy. In light of this, a language strategy is an endeavor undertaken by the community to achieve the optimal distribution of the language or languages that are spoken there (in accordance with goals that will be determined independently). Language planning and language policy are terms that are more commonly used in conjunction with one another.

A State, an area, a department, or a city could be considered public, or a company, a media conglomerate, or an association could be considered private. At times, they are regarded as variants of the same classification, and at other times they are used to differentiate between two levels of political action based on the languages used in a particular culture. Though Calvet (1987) argues that the opposite is not true, language planning and language policy are related concepts. It's possible that the political wording(s) selected will not always result in an exceptionally impressive legal-institutional execution.

France can serve as an example in this sense, as it has a long history of developing language policies. First and foremost, a language policy is a policy—a systematic approach to achieving a shared objective.

The main purpose of language policies is to manage user interests when there are different languages spoken on the same land.

Any group has the ability to create a language policy. The term "family language policies" is commonly used, or we can think of a community, such as the deaf or gypsies, making decisions about language policy.

However, the State and the family ultimately decide how policies are implemented. There is still a disagreement about the best term to use for carrying out a language policy. Should we use planning, development, or standardization? All three terms are found in sociolinguistic literature.

The main objective is to control one or more languages, both in their form and their use. This is referred to as "planning" by Anglo-Saxon researchers, "aménagement" based on social consensus for a collective project, or "normalization" popularized by Catalan sociolinguists in Spain.

According to Kilumba, Nkiko, et al. in 2013, language policy involves choosing languages and having a positive or negative attitude towards them. The study also suggests that language planning is about carrying out a predetermined policy to achieve specific goals.

In the Democratic Republic of Congo (DRC), French is used as the only officially recognized language in social, legal, political, and economic fields, while native languages are not given equal importance, leading to a gap between the privileged elite and the less informed majority.to support regional languages.

Various official documents attest that the nation's language policy has remained largely unchanged, except in the field of education. This policy was first instituted in 1906 by the Catholic Church during the Convention which mandated officials from the Diocese of Leopoldville in Kinshasa to convene in 1907 and determine the curriculum for the following year.

Van Keerberg (1985) stated that the educational program in the Democratic Republic of Congo was divided into three sections. The first section emphasized teaching essential skills like reading, writing, and arithmetic in the local dialect, along with basic geography, history, and mathematical operations. This method had been implemented for almost fifty years.

Nevertheless, it wasn't until the legislation of 1938 and 1948 and the insistence from the local community that French education was finally established. This pressure started with teaching in primary schools and later switched to French as the main language in third grade.

This system is still used today. In the first two years of primary school, students are taught in both languages. But from the third year on, French is the only language taught by missionaries, like Catholic Church members. In public schools, the national language is used for teaching, while in primary schools, it is the official language.

People often refer to ethnic languages in various ways, such as mother tongue, vernacular, minority language, local language, indigenous language, dialect, and more.

Unfortunately, these terms can sometimes suggest that ethnic languages are not as important.

Ethnic languages are usually learned naturally and are used for communication within different ethnic communities. However, they are gradually being replaced by international languages like French or English.

Historically, the Constitutions of the Democratic Republic of Congo have struggled to address the problem of ethnic languages. Besides the colonial charter, multiple constitutions were introduced from 1964 to 1974 that also had a major impact.

The lack of ethnic languages in this constitution is clear. The constitution suggested in 1999 of the DR Congo states that "the other languages of the country are part of the Congolese heritage, which the State protects and promotes." Still, it is not clear what role these languages play in the country.

There are many languages to think about, and discussing ethnic languages like this shows that lawmakers in the DR Congo have a tough choice with so many options. The Congolese Government must protect ethnic languages since they are in danger. The transitional constitution has added more ways to protect these languages. The lack of discussion about these languages by Congolese lawmakers highlights how much they are overlooked

The new constitution recognizes and prioritizes the languages of the DR Congo.

Seminars, workshops and conferences have been organised to solve the language problem, focusing mainly, as mentioned above, on the possible choice of a national language to become official as a replacement for French (Polome 1968; Bokamba 1976; Mutombo Huta-Mukuna 1987).

The sociolinguistics of the four vernacular languages has experienced notable shifts due to political, economic, and social influences. Lingala and Kiswahili have gained significance since the colonial era, with Lingala rising in prominence during the Mobutu regime and Kiswahili for multiple reasons.

There have been some studies recommending a single national language.

a. The choice of Lingala

According to well-documented article by Ntahwakuderwa (1987) argues that Lingala should be acknowledged as both the national and official language. This recognition could strengthen the current political leadership. The author points out how politicians play a key role in choosing a country's official language, using Kiswahili in Tanzania as an example and mentioning the Arusha Declaration, which provided equal educational chances for all citizens. Additionally, the article highlights other important benefits of Lingala, supported by various earlier studies, such as its ability to unite different communities and its broad usage across many areas of society.

1. Its use in Congolese music.
2. Its use in the Army.
3. Its use in Kinshasa, the capital city of the country.
4. The perception of many learners about Lingala language is that it is a relatively easy language.

b. The choice of Kiswahili

In another well-documented article, Kamwangamalu (1997) argues in favour of Kiswahili as the national language and second official language for the following reasons:

No one can claim ethnicity for this language in Congo because it was imported into Congo from Tanzania and Kenya and most of those who speak Kiswahili have another indigenous language that is not necessarily one of the four national languages. Kiswahili would therefore be perceived as a neutral language everywhere.

The country (DRC) could benefit from the Tanzanian language experience, which can be seen as a development success story; Kiswahili has a wider national and international distribution than the other national languages;

Even if the literary tradition of Kiswahili is no more developed than that of other languages in the DRC, it is developed outside the DRC with dictionaries, grammars, journals, poems, courses at foreign universities and broadcasts on foreign radio stations.

The Government would therefore spend less money on developing teaching materials for teaching Kiswahili.

As far as Lingala is concerned, without categorically rejecting Ntahwakuderwa's views, it is nevertheless important to put them somewhat into perspective:

Lingala is the main language in Congolese music, but it is important to note that other languages are also present. Kiswahili, for example, has been used by artists like Wendo and Bombenga. Additionally, phrases from various languages are still incorporated into the music;

b. Its use in the army is now shared with Kiswahili by the AFDL;

c. While using Lingala for the most part, the capital Kinshasa is gradually introducing other national languages, as can be seen in buses and other public places;

d. No language is entirely easier than others, depending on the psycholinguistic, sociolinguistic and pedagogical factors specific to the cases concerned.

With regard to Kiswahili, it is also important to recognize Kamwangamalu's argument and to define its limits:

1. The introduction of Kiswahili into Congo remains a topic of scholarly debate, particularly in relation to the timing of this introduction.
2. For some analysts, including Nkulu (1984), this introduction must have occurred long before the 19th century, given the prolific trade exchanges that would have taken place between the Katanga and Tanzanian chiefs, all of whom speak Kiswahili, several centuries earlier.
3. According to this thesis, the Congolese ethnic Kiswahili is effective, even though it is more recent than some others.
4. The experience and linguistic expansion of the language in foreign countries can have a certain impact on the domestic soil, but it should not be exaggerated, because national parameters are decisive for the adoption of a single official national language.
5. In terms of pedagogical advantage, it also remains limited in that the variety of Kiswahili to be taught in schools should not be far from common usage, even in its standardised form, bringing Kiswahili back to par with others languages.

In the final analysis, Kiswahili's real advantage over other languages remains its wider and internal distribution in the D R Congo, the political impact of which is undeniable.

Furthermore, the sociolinguistic status of the four Congolese languages has changed considerably in post-colonial Congo. During this period, Lingala had the status of a unique national language. A number of factors, including political, social and economic, have contributed to the rise of Lingala's sociolinguistic status, the most significant being its continual use in the military, music and the military coup of 1965 (Kutumisa, 1987; Malekani, etc.).

I.2.2.5. Studies on Mother tongues in the DRC

Malekani (2001) investigated on the mother tongue effect, of some students in Kisangani and the result of his research has shown that they are trilingual in Kiswahili, Lingala and French, as reflected in the MT effect total scores.

Using a foreign language like French by some Congolese students as a first language may seem strange at first. However, it is understandable because French is widely used in today's Congolese schools.

This conclusion requires that three MTs be considered instead of one in any contrastive analysis (CA), error analysis (EA), interlanguage (IL), or other applied linguistics studies covering the Congolese region that is the subject of this investigation.

Malekani (2002) carried out another sociolinguistic investigation aimed at examining the multilingualism of students from Kisangani and Kinshasa at the Faculty of psychological and Pedagogical sciences; and the study confirmed the dominant multilingualism of Kiswahili, Lingala and French.

A study by Tsengele (2012) explored how young learners develop their language skills and analytical thinking while learning English as a second language from infancy to age 12. The results disclosed that children whose parents are talkative demonstrate good command of language use and a broader range of vocabulary compared to those with reserved parents. Hence it is crucial for parents to actively engage in conversations with their children to promote language development.

Nsimambote (2014) suggested a quantitative method for identifying MTs and contrasted it with the scoring principle outlined by

Malekani (2012). His study concluded that the quantitative method assigns more accurate values to the base languages than the scoring principle. Five steps were defined in detail:

1st step: the researcher prepares questions that consist of items to identify MTs. 2nd step: the researcher submits these questions to the participants.

3rd step: the researcher presents the results by proportions exactly as the participants provided them. In case answers from different respondents diverge in terms of languages, they are grouped into single proportions.

4th step: classifying the grouped results of different items into their corresponding sociolinguistic parameters.

5th step: synthesizes the whole results of the study in a table of aggregate scores revealing the most dominant languages as the ones scoring the most basing on the scoring principle outlined by Malekani (2001).

Luzitusu (2021) conducted a study on mother tongue in the city of Kinshasa and found that young people in Kinshasa, especially in the Kindele district, acquire a different mother tongue from their parents. Such a mother tongue can be French or at least one of the national languages, while the mother tongue of the parents can be the Vernacular language.

In some cases, the researcher found that they are not only multilingual, but that these languages act as mother tongues for some of them by combining the following languages: French and Lingala or French and Swahili or French and Kikongo or Tshiluba, which were found to be dominant.

Kidinda (2021) investigated the influence of learners' mother tongue on the learning of English as a foreign language. He concluded that although the mother tongue is not important for an EFL learner, it still has an influence. As it has become a habit for students to speak in their mother tongue during breaks, this is a good example of students in some cases pronouncing English words as if it were their mother tongue.

Nsimambote (2023) provided a procedure to establish perfect mother tongue which implies languages used competently by speakers. He designed ten questions which are based on the two socio-psycholinguistic parameters termed: the speaker's emotional expression languages and easier languages of the speaker.

His illustrative study takes into account twenty students of the Department of media at the University of Kinshasa. Using the similar questions to assess the two parameters and basing on the quantitative procedure, the results of his study are presented in the table below: Note that the ten questions are kept in French for research reason.

LANGUAGE PROVIDED

Sociopsycho linguistic parameters	Related skills	Variables	Languages and proportions provided						
			Lingala	Kikongo	Ciluba	Kiswahili	French	English	Others
Languages of emotional expression of the speaker	Speaking	En quelle langue préférez-vous vous exprimer au tribunal pour mieux défendre ?	2	-	-	-	23	-	-
	Speaking	Lors d'une querelle, en quelle langue préférez-vous parler à la personne avec qui vous vous querellez ?	10	2	-	-	13	-	-
	Speaking	Lorsque vous êtes en difficulté et le secours est plus que nécessaire, en quelle langue criez-vous pour le secours ?	16	-	2	-	7	-	-
	Speaking	En quelle langue adressez-vous à votre partenaire pour exprimer vos intimités ?	-	-	1	-	19	3	-
	Speaking	En quelle langue lors de la communication, sentez-vous à l'aise et les idées viennent ?	5	-	1	-	17	2	-
	Listing	Quelle langue de vos émissions ou films préférés ?	-	-	1	-	21	3	-
	Writing	En quelle langue rédigez-vous avec beaucoup plus de confiance sans voir peur de commettre des erreurs d'orthographe?	2	-	1	-	18	1	-
Easier languages of the speaker	Reading	Lors des examens ou interrogations, en quelles langues réfléchissez-vous le plus souvent et qui vous aident à trouver aisément les réponses aux questions ?	4	-	1	-	19	-	-
	Speaking	En quelle langue vos camarades vous expliquent les cours en dehors de l'auditoire ?	5	-	-	-	17	-	-
	Speaking	En quelle langue préférez-vous que votre pasteur vous prêche à l'église ?	6	-	1	2	16	-	-
Total			**50**	**2**	**8**	**2**	**170**	**9**	**-**

The above table above provides an overview of the results of a survey questionnaire that the researcher conducted and has targeted students of the first year in the media Department.

In the first question, we see that when we asked about the language expressed in court, students use French mostly, followed by Lingala, with very little use of Swahili and French: French and Lingala, Kikongo, French and Kiswahili, and Lingala and Kiswahili;

For question 2, languages expressed in a quarrel, learners use more French language followed by Lingala and a few number of them mix languages when they speak: French and Lingala, Kikongo, French and Kiswahili and Kiswahili and Lingala and Ciluba and French.

In question 3 on the language of smooth expression, Lingala is the dominant language, followed by French and the lesser represented languages are: Kikongo, the combination of French and Lingala, French and Swahili, Lingala and Swahili;

Question 4 on language expressed in difficulty: Lingala is the most used language, followed by French,

Ciluba, the combination of French and Lingala and to a lesser extent Kikongo and the combination of French and Swahili;

In Question 5 on languages of intimacy, French is the language most commonly used by our respondents, in contrast to other languages that are used to the same extent: Lingala, Kikongo, Swahili, and the combination of French and Lingala, French and Swahili;

Question 6 Languages for reading quickly and fluently French is the most commonly used, followed by Lingala and the combination of French and Lingala, French and Swahili; Question 7 shows that French is an easy language to understand, followed by Lingala, the fusion of French and Lingala, French and Swahili, and finally Kikongo; In question 8, Screen languages of dreams, French dominates, while Lingala is in second place; In question 9, Languages of movies, French remains dominant, followed by a combination of French and Lingala, French and Swahili and, lastly, Kikongo; In question 10, Languages confided in while writing, French dominates all the other languages.

The total of different languages reveals French

with the highest scores (170). It is followed by Lingala with (50).Other languages such Kikongo, Swahili, Ciluba and English scoreless.

It is a surprise to notice that English, a foreign language scores higher than other national languages. Thus, the surveyed students were perfect multilinguals in both French and Lingala. These two languages can have impact on the learning and teaching of English as a foreign language.

I.3. Previous works on Mother tongues and the use of mother tongue in EFL classrooms

In the presentation of the previous works on the mother tongues in EFL classrooms, there are two groups to identify. The first group supports the idea to use the mother tongue in EFL classrooms while the second one is against the use of mother tongue in EFL classroom with English-only.

I.3.1. Previous works on Mother tongues

Atkinson (1987) is a pioneer or first contributor in the first group, he argues that very little attention is paid to the mother tongue in the teaching of English as a foreign language, and that this lack of methodological literature is probably responsible, at least in part, for the uncertainty that many teachers, both experienced and new, feel about it whether or not to use the mother tongue in the classroom.

Viewed in the context of EFL teaching approaches discussed in the preceding section, the use of the native language has undergone an oscillating movement from overuse to prohibition.

Atkison suggests that when we have to decide how much of the first language to use in class, a teacher should think about various factors like the student's level, the course level, the relationship with the teacher, and the part of the lesson.

Duff (1989) argues for the importance of the first language, saying that it influences how we think and how we approach foreign languages.

Atkinson (1987) confirms that a learner can use their first language if they cannot communicate in the second language.

Harbord (1992) explains that language acquisition involves not just learning to speak and think, but also developing a natural understanding of grammar through the first language.

Chomsky (1950s-1960s) proposed the theory of universal grammar, which differentiates between the deep and surface structures of language.

The deep structure is a basic structure present in all humans, while the surface structure is based on logical rules and changes.

This theory contests the structural view that language can be effectively studied solely through observable data without exploring its fundamental principles. Additionally, it posits that language acquisition encompasses more than merely producing correct utterances; it also requires using suitable language in diverse contexts.

Nonetheless, as the theory evolved, it became clear that its emphasis on an idealized standard form of language overlooks linguistic diversity.

Harbord recognised this as a mistake and called it the "emotional humanistic approach". He believed that language teaching should focus primarily on reducing students' anxiety by allowing them to use their native language in the early stages of learning. In this way, the native language is considered beneficial in the teaching process.

Auerbach (1993) gave the following situations as examples of situations that are beneficial to use L1:

a) Topic negotiation;

b) Classroom management;

c) Language analysis;

d) Explanation of grammatical rules;

e) Discussion of multicultural difficulties;

f) Explanation; g) Troubleshooting.

Similarly, Poulisse and Bongaerts (1994) studied the reasons why teachers code-switch when switching from L1 to L2 or vice versa during teaching. Code-switching can be used to meet language needs or achieve social/psychological goals, such as: B. Attracting students' attention, expressing emotions, changing the subject, etc

This refers to example (f), the guidelines of Auebarch (1993). In his study, Christovo (1996) emphasized the advantages of using the native language as a way to help learn a second language.

He also said that a student's native language shows how well they can handle different situations. However, relying only on the native language can make it harder to learn.

Therefore, teachers need to understand why students use their native language and use an ethnographic approach in their teaching.

When students rely solely on their native language without any limitations, it can slow down the learning process.

Therefore, teachers should understand why students use their L1 and use an ethnographic approach in their teaching.

This method suggests that students can learn both their native language and a second language at the same time, not just to connect words and structures, but also to help teachers understand how students process the second language and how social interactions change in the classroom.

Larson-Freeman (2000) states that using students' mother tongue in class helps them feel more comfortable, acts as a bridge between what they know and what they don't know, and clarifies the meaning of sentences in the new language.

Anton and Dicamilla (1999) explain that using the L1 is helpful for language learning because it helps learners have effective conversations when doing language activities that focus on meaning. John H.Bandura's cognitive theory, like Piaget in 1952, supports this idea.

Bamgbose (2000) stated that a big challenge for language planning in Africa is that many Africans have negative views about using African languages as the main languages for teaching.

These negative opinions are mostly because of the history of colonization and the low status given to African languages.

African languages have developed over time through exclusion, lack of knowledge, and the difficult experiences of their speakers. This has led to a pessimistic outlook, with many believing that English is the only way to receive a good education.

Some well-educated parents even believe that their children can only succeed by being educated in English, prioritizing job opportunities and social mobility.

Cook (2001) suggests that each aspect should be considered separately without the main focus being on avoiding the use of the first language.

It is also important to think about how well the first and second languages can be combined in the learning process. The fourth element involves students developing particular skills in the second language that they might need beyond the classroom.

Tang (2002) believes that using the first language in the classroom is helpful, even though it may not be the main way students communicate. It can support students' learning and help them understand different cultures and languages better.

Butzkamm (2003) also thinks it's important to use the first language to create a comfortable learning environment.

Many language teachers believe that using the first language can help students understand and apply new concepts, even if they initially prefer not to.

Researchers like Deller (2003), Gil and Greggio (2005), and Atkinson (1987) have found that teachers often end up using the mother tongue in the classroom. Deller (2003) argues that the first language can be useful for highlighting language differences and similarities, promoting spontaneity, fluency, group dynamics, and getting feedback from students.

However, Mello (2004) suggests that students may lose motivation to learn in the second language if both languages are used to teach the same subject, as they may rely too much on their native language.

They argue that using translation or the native

language can be an efficient technique in English language teaching. Lightbown and Spada (2006) also acknowledge the positive impact of the mother tongue on second language acquisition. The ongoing debate between proponents and opponents of using the mother tongue in language learning emphasizes the need for a more flexible approach in English as a Foreign Language (EFL) classrooms, particularly in countries like Asia and Africa, including South Africa and Algeria.

Seccato (2010) recommends that teachers should use both the first language (L1) and the second language (L2) in the classroom. This is because language teaching focuses more on writing than speaking. In today's globalized world, it is seen as old-fashioned to only teach one language and force children to learn it. Samadi (2011) states that teachers mainly use the L1 to explain grammar, translate vocabulary, manage the classroom, and teach lessons.

Students use the L1 to talk to teachers when they have trouble speaking in the L2. Using the L1 in foreign language classes also helps shy and nervous students feel more confident. It is important to let students use the L1 when they need to, instead of forcing them to use only the L2.

Al Hinai (2006) pointed out that using L1 has several benefits: It helps reduce learners' anxiety and creates a more relaxed learning environment.

It allows for the incorporation of learners' cultural background and knowledge in the classroom. It simplifies the process of checking understanding and giving instructions. Additionally, it helps in explaining the meaning of abstract words and highlighting the main differences in grammar and pronunciation between L1 and L2. Mahmutoglu and Kicir (2013) demonstrate how to effectively incorporate L1 in language teaching by:

1. Identifying the language (all levels).
2. Checking comprehension (all levels).
3. Giving instructions (early levels).
4. Cooperation among learners.
5. Discussions on teaching methodology (early level).
6. Presentation and reinforcement of language (mainly early levels).
7. Examination of meaning.

8. Testing.

Translanguaging is very important in English as a Foreign Language (EFL) classrooms at this level, according to Richards (2016).

It helps students understand and remember new words.

Ibrahim (2018) points out the differences between learning EFL and ESL, stressing the need for practice and exposure.

Unfortunately, in EFL countries, using English outside of class is not required. On the other hand, Mahmud (2018) supports bilingualism as the best way to teach English.

Ibrahim (2018) strongly argues that learning English as a foreign language is different from learning it as a second language and requires consistent practice and exposure. Sadly, in EFL countries, using English outside of class is not a must. In contrast, Mahmud (2018) strongly supports bilingualism as the most effective teaching method, using the native language to explain English.

This is to fight the common use of the grammar translation method in EFL classrooms. Kerr (2019) emphasizes the importance of using the students' first language in larger classes to create a good learning environment.

Burdujan (2020) highlights the importance of teachers' choices in allocating time for L1 and L2 in influencing students' L2 learning results.

Conversely, Tanriseven and Kirkgoz (2021) strongly advocate for the integration of L1 in ESL/EFL classrooms to improve learning and understanding, overcoming language barriers and making learning easier.

As scholars and writers delve into the best practices for using L1 in EFL classrooms, the frequency of its use varies based on factors like student age, learning goals, background, and proficiency level.

I.5.2. Previous works on the use of Mother tongues in EFL classrooms.

The second group consists of scholars who are

against incorporating L1 (mother tongue) in the classroom and offer justifications for their preference towards an exclusively English approach.

Leonard Bloomfield and William Skinner are two well-known figures in the field of language teaching. They introduced the Direct and Audio-Linguistic Methods in 1945. These methods focused heavily on learning patterns and structures, and then practicing and testing them until the student's responses became automatic.

The main idea behind these methods was that the first language (L1) and the second language (L2) should be treated as separate systems to avoid any potential learning difficulties, as suggested by Ellis (1997). Therefore, they advocated for the exclusion of L1 in English as a Foreign Language (EFL) classes. Experts believe that learning a second language follows a similar pattern to learning the first language.

Therefore, it is crucial to minimize the use of the native language when learning English as a foreign language. Philipson (1992) recommends five strategies for teaching

English in EFL classes.

The most effective strategy is to have an English-only policy. It is also believed that native English speakers make the best teachers.

Starting English education at an early age leads to better results, and the more English is taught, the better the outcomes. Using other languages too much can lower English proficiency.

Auerbach (1993) agrees with this idea, saying that the more students are exposed to English, the quicker they will learn it. By listening to and speaking English, students will absorb the language and start thinking in it, which helps them deal with emotional challenges and cultural differences. Students can really learn English only if they are motivated to use it regularly.

Ellis (1997) suggests that teaching the first language in the classroom is not advisable due to "transfer," which is when your native language affects how you learn a second language.

It is better to avoid using structures in the second language that do not exist in your native language. You cannot build habits in the second language without also having habits from your first language. Ellis calls this negative transfer.

One more reason to avoid using L1 in EFL classes is that you can only really learn a language by using it all the time. Krashen (1987) stresses the importance of exposing learners to the second language for acquisition.

Duff and Polio (1990) and Ellis (1997) also highlight the significance of using the target language in the learning process. On the other hand, Hawks (2001) suggests that the use of the native language should be carefully considered and may not always be the most effective method.

Prodromon (2001) goes as far as to describe the use of the native language as a hidden issue that needs to be addressed. Gabrielatos (2001) points out that using the first language in the classroom is a controversial topic.

According to Pacek (2003), using too much of your mother tongue can result in mistakes being transferred from your mother tongue to the second language, and relying too heavily on translation can make you think that the two languages are always exactly the same. One indication of communication issues is the continual use of translations.

Forman (2005) mentioned that in a situation where English is taught as a foreign language, students often have the same first language as their teacher. He wants to encourage the use of English beyond just an ESL setting because many classrooms have students who speak different languages.

Jones (2010) found that students learning a second language are more excited about learning and feel better when they participate in discussions and activities, whether alone or in groups. Sometimes, they may need to talk about the topic in their own language when working with a partner or in a group.

In conclusion, the researcher supports using the students' native language in English classes, as studies by UNESCO have shown that children learn best in their first language. This has been successful in countries like Tanzania, where they have recognized the importance of teaching English alongside the native language.

It is also practical to teach subjects like science

using a mix of the students' first language and English, especially in larger classes. This method is beneficial for students who speak multiple languages.

Teaching methodology courses and introducing scientific research in the student's native language can help them understand complex scientific concepts better.

This, in turn, can assist them in writing scientific papers such as essays and bachelor's theses. In multilingual African countries like Tanzania, where both Kiswahili and English are used in academic settings, including a local language alongside French can improve learning outcomes, especially if the dominant language is used.

Language is a powerful tool that connects people, conveys ideas, and shapes cultures. Our native language plays a crucial role in learning and understanding languages.

It is the first language we learn and the primary way we communicate within our community. The way we use our native language can greatly impact our ability to learn new languages and understand different cultures. Native language is essential for learning and understanding languages.

It serves as the basis for all other languages. Children learn their native language easily by simply listening to family members speak it. Being familiar with their first language helps them grasp how language works like grammar, sentence structure, and words. Studies indicate that students who are skilled in their first language do better when learning another language.

Language is not just about talking - it also involves discussing culture and identity. Speaking someone's first language is a way to show respect and appreciation for their background. Moreover, including the first language in the classroom can enhance students' grasp and memory of new material. When teachers explain ideas in students' first languages, it can make things clearer and boost their understanding. It also helps link what they already know with the new information.

Many writers and language experts think that mixing English with other languages is helpful because it offers more benefits. This is because English is not the primary language used in administration, particularly in education where most papers are written in French. Besides a few specific locations like study rooms, language schools, and churches, English is even less common in public institutions.

The language used in educational settings, especially in EFL or ESL classrooms, greatly affects the quality of teaching for students. It may be time for a change. A recent report from UNESCO, backed by the Ministry of Culture and the Arts and the Language Observatory, highlights the increasing focus on encouraging multilingualism in classrooms. This has caused a long-standing debate in our country about teaching methods in education. The Language Observatory aims to study how languages are used in Congolese society. Recent research indicates that as teaching methods advance, experts around the world are criticizing outdated approaches.

Each method has its drawbacks, and using our native language alongside English offers a chance to translate educational materials into the local language. This could help develop skilled language experts for our native languages.

It is important to understand that this approach does not involve directly translating English into the native language. Instead, it involves interpreting difficult parts of the language creatively. As Dodson (1972) previously mentioned, this idea can be expanded by systematically interpreting all relevant parts to be taught. A good solution might be to focus on analysing sentences with complex elements. The impact of language on individuals' experiences locally and globally is significant. In countries formerly colonized, language can either bring people together or divide them.

Experts from various language groups believe that language is a complex and personal way to connect people worldwide. Understanding different communities and environments is important. Linguists strive to protect language, while activists use it to unite people. Existentialists see language as a mirror of identity in society, politics, and culture. Educators find language to be a valuable tool for effective teaching.

Research by Mebratu in 2016 indicates that students who learn in their native language feel more confident, sharp, and better at communication and understanding academic material. Different groups of linguists view language as a personal and interconnected way to communicate.

It is essential for individuals to switch between local and global settings, especially when learning about marginalized communities.

Linguists may use language to preserve it, while activists use it to bring people together. Existentialists see language as a reflection of social, political, cultural, and linguistic identity. Educators consider language a strong and respectable tool for teaching (Mallikarjun, 2002).

In the discussions on mother tongue and English language teaching, scholars have been split into two groups: the one advocating the integration of mother tongue in the teaching of English as a foreign language and the other one that opposes this approach.

The researcher's contribution supports the feasibility of integrating mother tongue in teaching English as a foreign language. This allows multilingual students (learners) to get profit of their multilingual asset.

CHAPTER TWO: METHODOLOGY

There are four sections in this chapter. The first one is entitled population and sampling methods. The second one deals with the data of this dissertation. The third and fourth ones respectively target the description of the instruments used for data collection and methods used in analysing data.

II.1. Population and sampling methods
II.1.1. Population(participants)

In short, the people or things that satisfy certain requirements constitute the sample population, according to Polit and Hungler (1999).

As Kombo (2005) makes clear, a sample population is a subset of people that researchers study in order to learn more about a specific topic.

In statistics, the population is basically the whole group of people or things that we want to study. For example, if we are looking at students at a specific university, they would be the population. This makes it easier for researchers to focus on a specific group and get accurate results.

Sample size is just the total number of subjects or things under study when discussing sampling techniques.

Researchers can guarantee that the sample is representative of the whole population by using simple random sampling, which involves choosing a group of people at random from a wider population for study.

To create a random sample, systematic sampling, on the other hand, entails choosing items from a list that is ordered.

Sample strategies are important, in short, since they help researchers make sure that the population they are studying is correctly represented in their study. (Schukla 2020)

II.1.2. Sampling methods

Sample size is the number of participants in a study (McMillan & Schumacher, 2006).

Latpate and others (2021) explain that simple random sampling is a type of probability sampling in which researchers choose a smaller group of individuals from a larger group. Mujere (2016) defined sampling as a method of choosing a suitable sample or a representative section of a larger group to find out the traits or features of that entire group. In sampling, units from the population can include individuals (like students at a university or those taking a specific course), cases (such as recruitment agencies, organizations, or countries), and data points (like customer purchases at a supermarket or university applications in a nation).

A sampling method is a plan designed to ensure that the sample in a study closely resembles the population it was derived from (Denzin 2000).

This process involves several key terms including population sample sampling frame representativeness eligibility inclusion and exclusion criteria sample design bias sampling error performance analysis effect size and attrition.

As Yamane (1967) states the population refers to the entire target group while the sample is a subset of individuals actually studied by researchers (Zoltan Dornyei 2010). In accordance with Popplewell (2013) a sample is a collection of specific units that will be used to gather data.

To limit itself to a case study, the Department of media was chosen as it is part of the Faculty of Arts at the University of Kinshasa. In this department, the first year was specifically chosen. One-tenth (1/10) of the students were selected for a face- to -face interview which is defined as follows: a technique that requires a person known as the interviewer to ask questions generally in a face-to-face contact to the other person or persons (Kothari, 2004)

Participants interviewed were selected on the same day the researcher collected the survey questionnaire copies from students. They have been selected in terms of one per bench.

The interview was scheduled after a week. It took place in a café, where the interviewees were offered bottles of water during the conversation.

II.2. Data sources

According to Polkinghorne (2005) Data serve as a foundation on which findings are based. Data are collected from research participants using various data collection instruments.

Blaxter et al. (2006) identify four main instruments for data collection, namely: documents, interviews, observation and questionnaires.

This dissertation used three types of data, namely quantitative, qualitative and tests. The quantitative data were drawn thanks to the psycho-sociolinguistic questionnaire and the qualitative ones were drawn thanks to the interview. The statistical data consist of the scores obtained by the students learning English before using translanguaging and after using translanguaging. The test submitted to the participants reveal the positive impact of translanguaging method. The multi data of the current dissertation are presented in the table below:

Table 3: Multi data used in the dissertation

N^{th} data	Data 1 and Data 3	Data 2
Types	Quantitative	Qualitative
instruments	Tests Survey questionnaire	Interview

The table presents three types of data and three different instruments used to collect the needed data for this dissertation.

Description of the instruments

The socio-psycholinguistic questionnaire

As illustrated in the above table, three instruments were used to collect data. For data1, the survey questionnaire served as instrument. The interview allowed to collect data 2 and the tests submitted to the participants allowed to draw data 3.

One of the objectives of this dissertation is firstly to determine the perfect mother tongue of the participants according to the methodology suggested by Nsimambote (2023). The survey questionnaire consists of 17 questions divided into two parts: 2 identification variables and 15 research interest variables. The first part on identification variables consists of two closed questions: The first one concerns the gender of the respondent: male or female. Prospective participants had to choose one of these two options, but not both. The other question is related to the age of the participants. The following were options: 18-25; 26-29 and 30 +.They had to select their respective age ranks.

The second one on variables of research interest consists of 15 questions: easier languages of the speaker and languages of emotional expression of the speaker aged either from 18 to 25 years or aged 26 to 29 years being 30 years old or beyond.

The participant had the opportunity to select one of the ten questions in the second part, which focused on variables of research interest. These are questions assessing perfect mother tongue based on two social psycholinguistic parameters: the easier languages of speakers and the languages of emotional expression suggested by Nsimambote (2023).

The order of the questions runs as follows: The five questions in the beginning of questionnaire are closed-ended questions with seven possible answers, while the final question seeks to determine the answers to the questions relating to the four languages of the country: Ciluba (the national language), Kikongo (the national language of the country, which is the mother tongue of the participant) and Lingala (the lingua franca language, which is the official language of the applicant). The last question seeks to ascertain the answers to questions related to the foreign languages of the participant: French and English.

Unlike the first part, where the respondent had to choose as many languages as they could, five questions are focused on the participants' speaking skills. Unlike the second part, the participant did not have as many languages to choose as they could. These five questions are objectively used to check perfect mother tongues of a multilingual person's abilities. Nsimambote (2023).

The 6th question is the same as the first 5 questions as far as language choice is concerned. You have seven choices. The last one is the reading ability. The 7th, 8th, 9th and 10th questions are about listening. You have 7 choices similar to what you have in your research interests. The 10th and final question is about reading ability. Again, you have 7 choices. You will also see the language options. The 17 questions are about the social psycholinguistic questionnaire and are attached as Appendix A.

Interview questions

As already mentioned, the researcher invited few students to an interview in a café which means out of 250 students in total, 25 have been selected representing one tenth.

The choice of this setting can be explained by the fact that the researcher wanted to enjoy the comfort of a café, which also had psychological significance. The same ten questions of research interest were used in the interview; they were all open-ended.

The researcher estimated the age of the respondents since gender did not have to be asked. All ten questions are shown in Appendix B.

The test

In this dissertation, classical test theory was applied. This theory is about test scores which introduces three concepts (1) test score (2) true score and (3) error score (Hambleton and Jones, 1993).

Vincent and Shammugan (2020) state that test scores reflect the actual abilities of each examinee, but these scores can be affected by errors, making them either higher or lower. To simplify the scoring process, researcher focused on micro-skills rather than the four main language skills. These micro-skills include grammar, vocabulary, pronunciation, and spelling (Aydogan and Akbarov, 2014).

This dissertation focuses on a specific grammar lesson to test participants using the translanguaging method. Participants underwent two tests: the first with traditional English teaching and the second with multilingual teaching through translanguaging. The results of the two tests demonstrated the positive impact mother tongues of the participants.

The grammar lessons were chosen based on Auerbach's ideas (1993), using micro competence and scores to match responses correctly. The teaching assistant was assigned to teach the lesson on reported speech to the participants. He emphasized these main points:

- Defining reported speech by specifying both the direct and indirect ones.
- Some exercises on putting the direct speech into indirect one and vice-versa by illustrating the different changes.
- Cover all the types of message, namely statements,

questions, imperative, exclamative and the ones with nominal sentences.

He used two teaching methods: monolingual teaching and multilingual one. In monolingual teaching, he used the English language only while in the multilingual one; he used two languages that were established as perfect mother tongues of the participants. It is important to mention that both teachings took place after the establishment of the participants' perfect mother tongues.

In multilingual teaching, the researcher instructed the teaching assistant to apply the perfect mother tongues while displaying the following situations identified by Auerbach (1993) explanation of grammatical rules; directions; and error resolution. The perfect mother tongues were used by code swiching from one to another (Poulisse and Bongaerts (1994).

Wearing a sociolinguist's cap, the researcher collaborated with him by testing the learners, on the first week with monolingual test and the second one with multilingual one. The test was graded over ten (/10). The test and some hard copies of the test of some participants are attached in this dissertation.

II.4.4. Methods used in data interpretation

This section should clearly outline the theoretical and experimental techniques and materials used in your research. This allows any reader to replicate your work and achieve the same results. Be clear, thorough, and to the point: include only necessary information. For instance, cite a source for a specific method instead of detailing every aspect as explained by Dawit (2020). Besides, this section should also present the study's findings using figures and tables effectively. According to Wilkinson (1991), this part must display results in a clear and logical manner to emphasize possible implications. Use a mix of text, tables, and figures to summarize the data, highlight key trends, and show relationships between different data points. Ensure that figures are well-designed, clear, and easy to interpret. Captions for figures should be brief but informative enough to understand the figures without needing to refer back to the text.

This model of data collection and analysis enables

researchers to update themselves and present the results of their research in a slightly more systematic way, in line with the realities of the modern world, and to develop high-level thinking skills.

This study has used double sequential explanatory model of mixed methods.

Diagram 1: The illustration of a double sequential explanatory model (the multiphase design) used in the study as adapted from Creswell and Plano Clark (2011)

The mixed methods design in this dissertation follows the approach used by Creswell and Plano Clark (2018), which is also referenced by Angell and Townsend (2021).It consists of a double sequential explanatory model of this pattern.

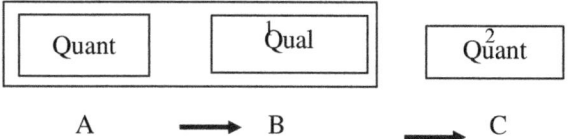

sequences in that order.

1 and 2 A consisted of a survey and B was an interview. The results of the later served as a follow up study to A. C consisted of another quantitative study statistically based which illustrates or explains the findings of A and B.

This sketch designed by Creswell shows us the different phases to follow when collecting data in a scientific study and which we have tried to apply in our work, as you will see in the following pages, mainly at the level of data analysis.

The diagram 2 for this model is below:

C) *Used in the multiphase design (mixed methods) of the study*

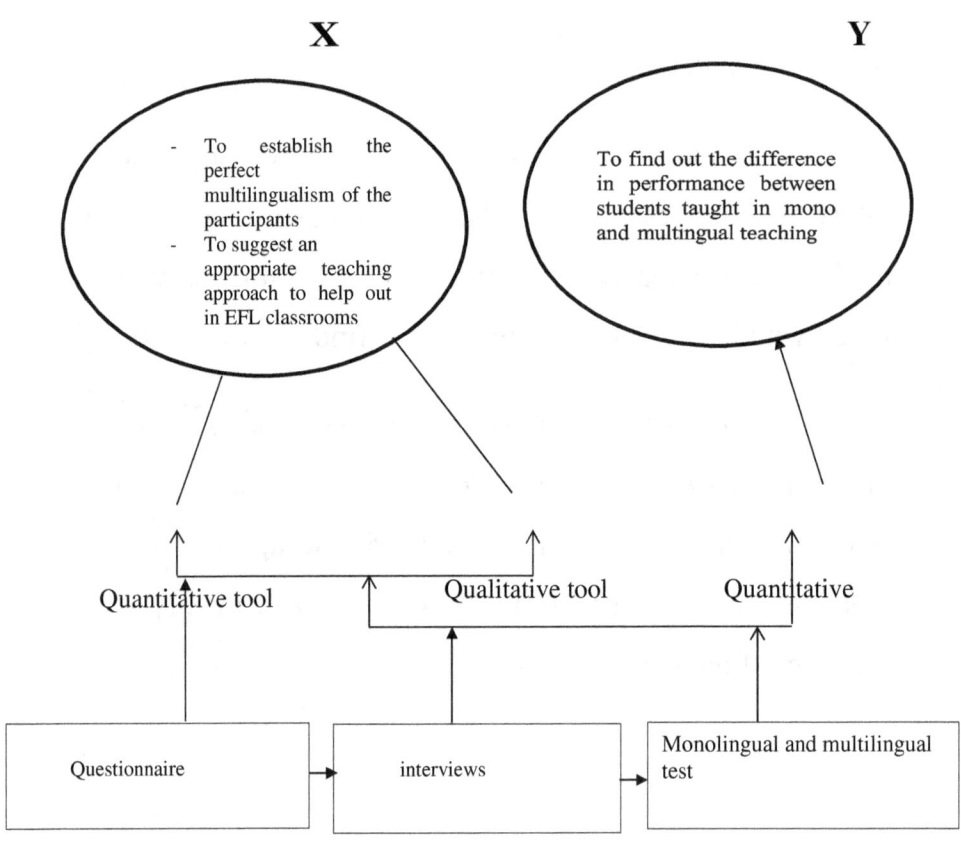

The test was related to the grammar lesson presented below:

Grammar lesson for L1 LMD students of media on direct and indirect speech

(also known as indirect speech)

Direct Speech	Reported Speech
Kalala: *"I am cooking dinner Mboma."*	**Mboma**: *"Kalala said he was cooking dinner."*

So most often, the reported speech is going to be in the past tense, because the original statement, will now be in the past!

Take

Be careful with the use of your ***commas/inverted commas*** and (quotation) *report

"I often play tennis," she said.

"I often play tennis!" she shouted.

"Do you often play tennis?" she asked. She

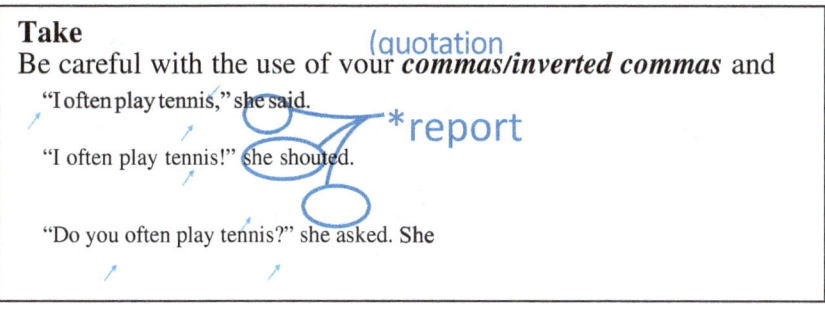

*We will learn about reporting verbs in part 2 of this lesson, but for now we will just use *said/told*

as our reporting verbs.

Take note: the structures of *say and tell* are different:

1. when using *say*, we *cannot include* an object:

He said that (that) he was leaving.

2. when using *tell*, we *must include* an object:

*He told **Claude** (that) he was leaving.*

Usually, the reported statement is *one tense back* from the direct speech statement:

DIRECT SPEECH REPORTED SPEECH

Present Simple   **Past Simple**

"I often **play** tennis," she said.	She said (that) she often **played** tennis.
Present Continuous "We **love going** camping," he said.	**Past continuous** He said (that) they **loved going** camping.

Past Simple "I **stayed** in Kinshasa," he said.	**Past Perfect** He told me (that) he **had stayed** in Kinshasa.
Present Perfect "Francine **has eaten**," Robert said.	**Past Perfect** Robert said (that) Francine **had eaten**.
***Past Perfect** "Our taxi **had just arrived**," Joseph said.	***Past Perfect** Joseph told me their taxi **had just arrived**.
Present Perfect Continuous "Ryan **has been studying**," Mila said.	**Past Perfect Continuous** Mila said (that) Ryan **had been studying**.
Past Continuous "They **were singing**," she said.	**Past Perfect Continuous** She said (that) they **had been singing**.

***mustn't** can also remain unchanged in reported speech.

TAKE NOTE:

1. If the direct speech statement includes the any of the following modal verbs, ***they do not change*** when transformed into reported speech:

may, might, would, should, ought to

DIRECT SPEECH	REPORTED SPEECH
might	**might**
"I **might** buy a new car," said Maguy.	Maguy told me (that) he **might** buy a new car.
should	**Should**
"They **should** try the local cuisine," Leon said.	Leon said (that) they **should** try the local cuisine.

2. If the situation in the reported statement ***hasn't***

changed and is still true in the present, the reporting verb ***can remain in the same form***:

DIRECT SPEECH	REPORTED SPEECH
"My son ***is*** four years old," said Olivier.	*Olivier said (that) his son ***is*** four years old.
"Vegetables ***are*** good for a healthy diet," he said.	*He said (that) vegetables ***are*** good for a healthy diet.

*the above examples are still correct if you ***do*** convert the verbs to their past tenses: Olivier said (that) his son ***was*** four years old.

He said (that) vegetables ***were*** good for a healthy diet.

3. When we talk about places, if the direct speech statement includes ***here***, it changes to ***there*** in the reported version:

DIRECT SPEECH	REPORTED SPEECH
here	**there**
"Have you been ***here***	*David asked if I had been ***there*** before.

before," asked David.	
"They buy the best cassava leaves **here**," said Olga.	Olga said (that) they bought the best cassava leaves **there**.

*The above examples also depend on **where** the reported statement is being made. For example, if the above reported statements are being made while the person reporting the information is still in the same place where the conversation took place, the reported speech could also be:

David asked if I had been **here** before.

Olga said (that) they bought the best cassava leaves **here**.

In reported Speech, **adverbs of time also change** as follows:

DIRECT SPEECH	REPORTED SPEECH
today(tonight) "Didi is going to the beach **today**," she said.	**that day(that night)** She said (that) Didi was going to the beach
tomorrow "We will fix it **tomorrow**," he said.	**that day, the next day, the day after, the following day** He said (that) they would fix it **the next day**.
yesterday "I went **yesterday**," she said.	**the day before, the previous day** She said (that) she had been **the day before**.

last week	The week before
"Bavon paid him **last week**," he said.	He told me (that) Bavon had paid him **the week before**.
this morning	that morning
"I washed my car **this morning**," Mila said.	Mila said (that) she had washed her car *that morning*.
next (Wednesday)	the following (Wednesday)
"We are leaving **next Wednesday**," Patrick said.	Patrick said (that) they were leaving *the following Wednesday*.
ago	before
"I arrived here a long time **ago**," he said.	He said (that) he had arrived there a long time *before*.

Task 1

Change the following sentences from direct speech into reported speech:

1. "I am always in a bad mood on Monday mornings," said Paul.

2. "They were working last week," she said.

3. "I have been to DRC," said Evelyn.

4. "Isabell will give you a lift to the airport

tomorrow," he said.

5. "We had already eaten before we arrived so we didn't taste the food," said Simon.

6. "I can't come to the party tonight, I have to study," she said.

7. "You mustn't go near that cliff edge, it's dangerous!" said Zoey.

8. "You weren't looking well yesterday," Luke said.

Task 2

Transform the following sentences from direct speech into reported speech:

1. "I am always in a bad mood on Monday mornings," said Claude.

Brian said (that) he is/was always in a bad MOOd on Monday MOrnings.

2. "They were working last week," she said.

She said (that) they had been working the week before.

3. "I have been to Zimbabwe," said Evelyn.

Evelyn said (that) she had been to DRC.

4. "Isabell will give you a lift to the airport tomorrow," he said.

He said (that) Isabel would give me a lift to the airport tomorrow.

(the next day/the following day/the day after)

5. "We had already eaten before we arrived so we didn't taste the food," said Simon.

Simon said they had already eaten before they had arrived, so they didn't taste the food.

6. "I can't come to the party tonight, I have to study," she said.

She said (that) she couldn't come to the party that night, she had to study.

7. "You mustn't go near that erosion, it's dangerous!" said Mike.

Mike said (that) I shouldn't go near that , it's dangerous.

8. "You weren't looking well yesterday," Luke said.

(last night/last Saturday night)

Luke said (that) **I** hadn't been looking well the day before. (the previous day)

Task 3

Change the following sentences from reported speech into direct speech. Pay attention to the punctuation required when using direct speech.

1. She said that they had paid the bill.
2. Kelly said she was so tired of working every weekend.
3. He said their house had been for sale for six months.
4. Mark said that he had gone surfing the weekend before.

5. Max said he could help us move flats tomorrow.
6. My grandfather said that he had already had a baby by my age.
7. Bob said that Georges hates going to the concert on weekends.
8. He said that he had loved his trip to Kisangani the year before.

Task 4

Change the following sentences from reported speech into direct speech. Pay attention to the punctuation required when using direct speech.

1. She said that they had paid the bill.

"They have paid the bill," she said.

2. Kelly said she was so tired of working every weekend.

"I aM SO tired of working every weekend," Kelly said.

3. He said their house had been for sale for six months.

"Our house has been for sale for six MOnths," he said.

4. Mark said that he had gone surfing the weekend before.

"I went surfing last weekend," said Mark.

5. Max said he could help us move flats tomorrow.

"I can help you MOve flats toMOrrow," said Max.

6. My grandfather said that he had already had a baby by my age.

"I had already had a baby by your age," said MY grandfather.

7. Bob said that Georges hates going to the concert on weekends.

"Hadey hates going to the beach on weekends," said Greg.

8. He said that he had loved his trip to Kisangani the year before.

"I loved MY trip to Kisangani last year," he said.

Lingala Version of grammar lesson.

Liteya ya grammaire mpo na bayekoli ya L1 LMD ya media na elobeli ya direct mpe indirect

Elobeli ya Semba

Kalala: "*Nazali kolamba bilei ya mpokwa Mboma.*"

Donc mingi mingi, discours oyo elobami ekozala na temps passé, po déclaration originale, ekozala sikoyo na temps passé!

Tóye

Keba na kosalela ba virgule na yo/virgule (ba

Alobaki boye:
"Mbala mingi nabɛtaka tennis. *ba

"Mbala mingi nabɛtaka tennis!" agangaki na ye.

---

* .Tokoyekola na ntina ya ba verbe ya kopesa lapolo na eteni ya 2 ya liteya oyo, kasi mpo na sikoyo

tokosalela kaka alobaki/ayebisaki

lokola ba verbes na biso ya kopesa lapolo.

Tóyeba: ba structures ya koloba na koyebisa ekeseni :

3. ntango tozali kosalela koloba, tokoki te kokɔtisa eloko moko:

    Alobaki ete (ete) azali kokende.

4. tango tozali kosalela tell, esengeli totia eloko moko:

    Ayebisaki Claude (ete) azali kokende.

Mbala mingi, maloba oyo elobami ezali na ntango moko nsima na maloba

ya elobeli ya semba:

LILOBA YA DIRECT	ELOBIMALOBA
Présent Simple ya pete	**Eleka Pete**
Alobaki boye: "Mbala mingi nabɛtaka tennis	*Alobaki boye: "Mbala mingi nabɛtaka tennis.*

Présent Continu Alobaki boye: "Tolingaka kokende kosala bakaa."	**Présent Continu** Alobaki boye: "Tolingaka kokende kosala bakaa."
Past Simple Alobaki boye: "Natikalaki na Kinshasa.	**Past Simple** Alobaki boye: "Natikalaki na Kinshasa.
Present ya kokoka Robert alobaki boye: "Francine asili kolya.	**Present ya kokoka** Robert alobaki boye: "Francine asili kolya."
***Eleka Parfait** Joseph alobaki boye: "Taxi na biso eutaki kokóma.	***Eleka Parfait** Joseph alobaki boye: "Taxi na biso eutaki kokóma.
Présent Parfait Continu Mila alobaki boye: "Ryan azali koyekola. **Past Continu** Alobaki boye: "Bazalaki koyemba.	**Présent Parfait Continu** Mila alobaki boye: "Ryan azali koyekola. **Past Continu** Alobaki boye: "Bazalaki koyemba.

Ba verbes modal mosusu ebongwanakantango ozali kosalela elobeli oyo elobelami, ndenge elandi:

LILOBA YA DIRECT	ELOBIMALOBA
Akoki	Akoki
Emma alobaki boye: "Nakoki kobɛta mai malamu Alobaki boye: "Bakoki kobima te	Emma alobaki (ete) akokaki kobɛta mai malamu.

	Ye alobaki (ete) bakokaki kobima te.
Ako Bobo alobaki boye: "Nakosukola basaani." Alobaki boye: "Nakopota mbangu mosika mpenza te."	**Ako** Bobo alobaki (ete) akosukola basaani. Ye alobaki (ete) akokima mosika mingi te.
Esengeli (mpo na mokumba). Alobaki boye: "Tosengeli kokende."	**esengelaki kosala bongo** Ye ayebisaki ngai (ete) basengelaki kokende.
esengeli te(mpo na epekiseli). Alobaki boye: "Osengeli kosimba likambo yango te."	***esengeli te (esengeli te)** Ayebisaki ngai (ete) nasengeli te kosimba yango. Ayebisaki ngai (ete) esengeli nasimba yango te.

***esengeli te**ekoki mpe kotikala kobongwana te na elobeli oyo elobami.

TOSALA LISAKOLI:

4. Soki maloba ya elobeli ya semba ezali na moko ya ba verbe modaux oyo elandi, ebongwanaka te ntango ebongwanaka na elobeli oyo epesamaki lapolo:

ekoki, ekoki, elingaki, esengeli, esengeli

LILOBA YA DIRECT	LILOBA OYO BALOBI
ekoki	ekoki
Maguy alobaki boye: "Nakoki kosomba motuka ya sika.	Maguy ayebisaki ngai (ete) akoki kosomba motuka ya sika.
Esengeli	Esengeli
Leon alobaki boye: "Basengeli komeka bilei ya mboka."	Leon alobaki (ete) esengeli bameka cuisine ya mboka.

5. Soki likambo oyo ezali na maloba oyo epesamaki lapolo ebongwanaki te mpe ezali kaka solo na ntango oyo, verbe ya kopesa lapolo ekoki kotikala na lolenge moko:

LILOBA YA DIRECT	LILOBA OYO BALOBI
Olivier alobaki boye: "Mwana na ngai ya mobali azali na mbula minei.	*Olivier alobaki (ete) mwana na ye azali na mbula minei.
Alobaki boye: "Ngunda ezali malamu mpo na kolya malamu."	*Alobaki (ete) ndunda ezali malamu mpo na bilei ya malamu.

*ba exemples oyo ezali likolo ezali kaka correct soki osali convertir ba verbes na ba temps passés na yango : Olivier alobaki (ete) mwana na ye ya mobali azalaki na mbula minei.

Alobaki (ete) ndunda ezalaki malamu mpo na bilei ya malamu.

6. Tango tolobeli bisika, soki déclaration ya discours direct esangisi awa, ebongwanaka kuna na version oyo epesameli rapport:

LILOBA YA DIRECT	LILOBA OYO BALOBI
awa	kuna
David atunaki boye: "Ozalaki awa liboso."	*David atunaki soki nazalaki kuna liboso.
Olga alobaki boye: "Basombaka nkasa ya manioko oyo eleki malamu awa.	Olga alobaki (ete) basombaki nkasa ya manioko ya malamu koleka **kuna**.

*Bandakisa oyo ezali likolo etali pe esika oyo maloba oyo elobami ezali kosalama. Na ndakisa, soki maloba oyo tolobeli awa na likoló ezali kolobama ntango moto oyo azali koyebisa makambo yango azali naino na esika oyo lisolo yango esalemaki, diskur oyo elobami ekoki mpe kozala:

David atunaki soki nazalaki awa liboso.

Olga alobaki (ete) basombaki nkasa ya manioko ya malamu koleka awa.

Na Liloba oyo epesameli lapolo, ba adverbes ya tango ebongwanaka pe boye :

LILOBA YA DIRECT	ELOBIMALOBA
lelo(na butu ya lelo) *Alobaki boye: "Didi azali kokende na libongo lelo."*	oyo mokolo(butu wana). *Alobaki (ete) Didi azalaki kokende na libongo*
lobi *Alobaki boye: "Tokobongisa yango lobi."* **lobi eleki** *Alobaki boye: "Nakendeki lobi.*	*mokolo wana.* **mokolo oyo elandi, mokolo oyo elandi, mokolo oyo elandi** *Alobaki (ete) bakobongisa yango mokolo oyo ekolanda*
poso eleki *Alobaki boye: "Bavon afutaki ye na pɔsɔ eleki."*	**mokolo moko liboso, mokolo oyo elekaki** *Alobaki (ete) azalaki mokolo moko liboso.*
na ntongo ya lelo *Mila alobaki boye: "Nasukolaki motuka na ngai na ntongo ya lelo.*	Poso oyo eleki Ayebisaki ngai (ete) Bavon afutaki ye poso moko liboso. **na ntongo wana** *Mila alobaki (ete) asukolaki motuka na ye na ntongo wana*
ekoya (mokolo ya misato) *Patrick alobaki boye: "Tozali kokende mokolo ya misato oyo* *ekoya."*	**oyo elandi (mokolo ya misato)** *Patrick alobaki (ete) bazalaki kokende mercredi oyo elandaki*
eleki *Alobaki boye: "Nakómaki awa kala mpenza.*	**liboso** *Alobaki (ete) akomaki kuna kala* *liboso.*

Mosala 1

Bobongola masakola oyo elandi uta na maloba ya semba kino na maloba oyo epesameli lapolo:

9. Paul alobaki boye: "Nazalaka ntango nyonso na ezalela ya mabe na mokolo ya mibale na ntɔngɔ."
10. Alobaki boye: "Bazalaki kosala na pɔsɔ eleki.
11. Evelyn alobaki boye: "Nakendeki na RDC.
12. Alobaki boye: "Isabell akopesa yo ascenseur mpo na kokende na libándá ya mpɛpɔ lobi."
13. Simon alobaki boye: "Tosilaki kolya liboso tókóma yango wana tomekaki bilei yango te."
14. Alobaki boye: "Nakoki koya na fɛti te na mpokwa ya lelo, nasengeli koyekola."
15. "Osengeli te kopusana penepene na mopanzi wana ya libanga, ezali likama!" alobaki Zoey.
16. Luka alobaki boye: "Ozalaki komonana malamu te lobi.

Mosala ya 2

Bobongola masakola oyo elandi uta na maloba ya semba kino na maloba oyo epesameli lapolo:

(mokolo oyo elandi/mokolo oyo elandimokolo/mokolo oyo elandi)

9. Claude alobaki boye: "Nazalaka ntango nyonso na ezalela ya mabe na mokolo ya mibale na ntongo."

   Claude alobaki (ete) azali/azalaki ntango nyonso na ezalela ya mabe na mokolo ya mibale na ntongo.

10. Alobaki boye: "Bazalaki kosala na pɔsɔ eleki.

    Alobaki (ete) bazalaki kosala poso moko liboso.

11. Evelyn alobaki boye: "Nakendeki na Zimbabwe.

    Evelyn alobaki (ete) azalaki na RDC.

12. Alobaki boye: "Isabell akopesa yo ascenseur mpo na kokende na libándá ya mpɛpɔ lobi."

    Alobaki (ete) Isabel akopesa ngai ascenseur na aéroport lobi.

13. Simon alobaki boye: "Tosilaki kolya liboso tókóma yango wana tomekaki bilei yango te."

    Simon alobaki ete basilaki kolya liboso bákóma, yango wana bamekaki bilei yango te.

14. Alobaki boye: "Nakoki koya na fɛti te na mpokwa ya lelo, nasengeli koyekola."

Alobaki (ete) akokaki koya na feti te na butu wana, asengelaki koyekola.

15. "Osengeli te kopusana pene na érosion wana, ezali likama!" alobaki Mike.

Mike alobaki (ete) nasengeli te kokende pene na yango, ezali likama.

16. Luka alobaki boye: "Ozalaki komonana malamu te lobi.

(butu eleki/samedi eleki na butu)

Luka alobaki (ete) nazalaki komonana malamu te mokolo moko liboso. (mokolo oyo elekaki)

Mosala ya 3

Bobongola bafraze oyo elandi uta na maloba oyo epesamaki lapolo kino na maloba ya semba. Tyá likebi na bilembo ya bopemi oyo esengeli ntango ozali kosalela maloba ya semba.

9. Alobaki ete bafutaki mbongo yango.
10. Kelly alobaki ete azalaki kolɛmba mingi kosala

wikende nyonso.

11. Alobi ndako na bango esili kotɛkama banda sanza motoba.

12. Mark alobaki ete akendaki kosala surf na wikende liboso.

13. Max alobaki ete akoki kosalisa biso tokende kofanda na ba appartements lobi.

14. Nkoko na ngai ya mobali alobaki ete asilaki kobota na mbula na ngai.

15. Bob alobaki ete Georges ayinaka kokende na concert na bawikende.

16. Alobaki ete asepelaki mingi na mobembo na ye na Kisangani mbula moko liboso.

Mosala ya 4

Bobongola bafraze oyo elandi uta na maloba oyo epesamaki lapolo kino na maloba ya semba. Tyá likebi na bilembo ya bopemi oyo esengeli ntango ozali kosalela maloba ya semba.

9. Alobaki ete bafutaki mbongo yango.

Alobaki boye: "Bafuti mbongo yango.

10. Kelly alobaki ete azalaki kolɛmba mingi kosala wikende nyonso.

Kelly alobaki boye: "Nalɛmbi mingi kosala wikende nyonso."

11. Alobi ndako na bango esili kotɛkama banda sanza motoba.

Alobaki boye: "Ndako na biso esili kotɛkama banda sanza motoba."

12. Mark alobaki ete akendaki kosala surf na wikende liboso.

Mark alobaki boye: "Nakendaki kosala surf na wikende eleki.

13. Max alobaki ete akoki kosalisa biso tokende kofanda na ba appartements lobi.

Max alobaki boye: "Nakoki kosalisa yo okende kofanda na bandako mosusu lobi."

14. Nkoko na ngai ya mobali alobaki ete asilaki kobota na mbula na ngai.

Nkoko na ngai alobaki boye: "Nasilaki kobota mwana na mbula na yo.

15. Bob alobaki ete Georges ayinaka kokende na concert na bawikende.

Greg alobaki boye: "Hadey ayinaka kokende na libongo na bawikende.

16. Alobaki ete asepelaki mingi na mobembo na ye na Kisangani mbula moko liboso.

Alobaki boye: "Nasepelaki mingi na mobembo na ngai na Kisangani na mbula eleki."

The researcher used these questions to ask students to answer, ensuring they truly understood the lesson. To his surprise, most of them were eager to answer when the grammar lesson was taught in French and somewhat in Lingala. There was a noticeable level of participation from them

CHAPTER THREE: RESULTS

Six sections make up the current chapter which essentially presents the research results and findings. The first one provides a description of the different codes used before uploading the excel data set to the IBM SPSS Statistics version 20. The second one gives the presentation of the survey questionnaire data results while the third one targets the interview ones. The fourth one deals with the results of both monolingual and multilingual tests. The fifth one concerns interpretation of the research results and the sixth and last presents findings.

To start with, the study targeted one hundred and fifty participants who received the questionnaire copies during the survey. After collecting their written copies, it was noticed that only one hundred participants were returned their copies with responses. This proportion of 66.6% is acceptable for research. In the interview, one tenth of those returned the written copies that is to say fifteen participants were scheduled to respond verbally what they had written in their copies. This interview was semi-structured to get more relevant data concerning the current study.

III.1 Coding

In this section, the different codes used in the two Excel Spreadsheet data set for survey questionnaire and interview are identified. The two data set are presented as follows:

Survey Data set

Gender	Age	Languages used in a court	Languages used in a quarrel
1	1	5	1
1	1	5	1
1	1	15	15
1	1	5	1
2	1	5	5
2	1	1	1
2	1	5	15
2	1	5	5
2	1	6	5
2	1	5	5
2	1	1	1
2	1	1	1
2	1	4	4
2	1	5	5
1	1	5	1
2	1	5	1
2	1	1	1
2	1	5	1
2	1	1	5

As shown in the above two tables of data set, numbers in both survey and interview data represented sub variables depending on the concerned variables. They are identified as follows:

Gender

1. Masculine
2. Feminine
3. Age

1: 18 to 25

2: 26 to 29

3: 30 over

>For specific variables related to languages. The following coding was applied:

1: Lingala

2: Kikongo

3: Ciluba

4: Kiswahili

5: French

6: English

7: Other languages to be specified by the participants.
15: Lingala and French

45: Kiswahili and French
56:French and English

125: Lingala, Kikongo and French
126: Lingala, Kikongo and English

127: Lingala, Kikongo and other

languages 145: Lingala, Kiswahili and French

Other variables were not coded for evident reasons such as the variable concerning the views of the respondents on multilingualism in teaching or learning English.

III.2 Survey data analysis

This section is subdivided into two subsections. The first one presents survey data identification variables and the second one deals with the survey research interest variables.

III.2.1 Survey data identification variables

Two variables were concerned for identification variable in the survey.

They are namely gender and age.

III.2.1.1 Gender

After analysing the results of the survey, it is disclosed that female students dominate over male students. The proportions of female students representing (63%) is nearly the double of male students as illustrated below:

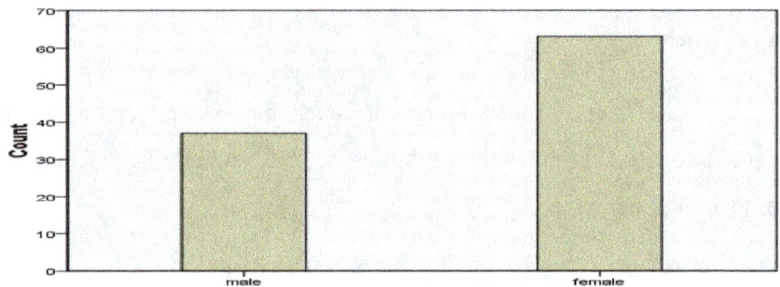
Figure 1: Gender

As observed, the department of communication of the University of Kinshasa is more preferred by female students than male students. The proportions of (37%) of males are not to be minimised. The study sample is not homogenous as both male students and female students have participated.

III.2.1.2 Age

For this variable, the results produce two different ranges of age. The one ranging from 18 to 25 is made of the respondents with the proportions of (96%). The remaining participants belong to the age group ranging from 26 to 29.

Figure 2: Age

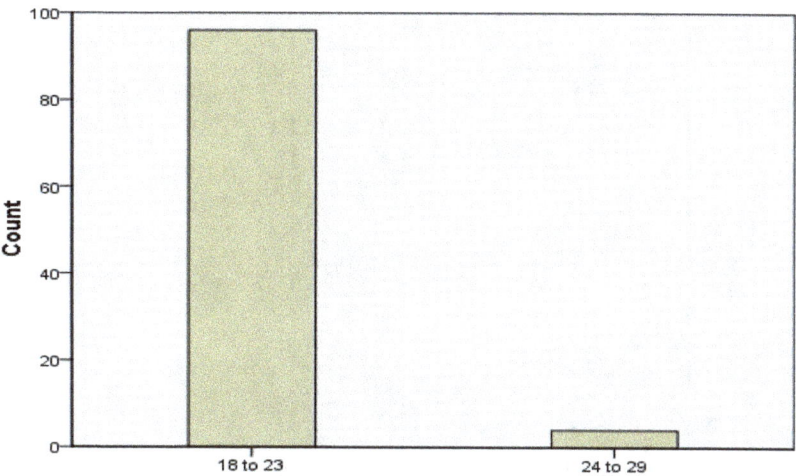

There are not participants who selected the age ranging from 30 years over. It is clear that all the participants are less than 30 years old.

III.2.2 Survey data research interest variables
III.2.2.1 Languages used in a court

This item targeted the languages expressed in a court by the participants. The analysis reveals French at the top as most the particpants(77%) selected it. It is followed by Lingala with nineteen participants or (19%).

At the third position, occurs Lingala and French and the remaining languages have the similar scores indicated in the following figure.

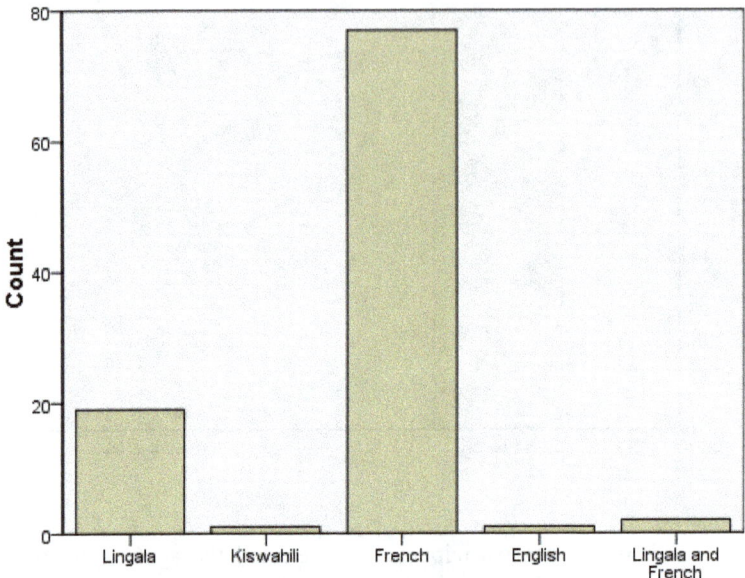

Figure 3: Languages expressed in a court

As a matter in the Congolese courts, a guilty person is supposed to use the language he or she express the best. The choice of Lingala, Lingala+French and Kiswahili is justifiable. It is astonished to notice that one respondent selected English which is the official language of the country. This can be justifiable for foreigners or Congolese who grew up in English speaking countries. In this case, an interpreter is needed. French scores the most as it is the official language used in different institutions as is used in justice.

None of the participants mentioned Kikongo, Ciluba and vernacular languages. These languages are also allowed by the court if the guilty person can express the best by using them. Other foreign languages such as Spanish, Portuguese, and Russian and so on are also allowed, but interpreters are needed.

III.2.2.2 Languages used in a quarrel

Concerning this variable, Lingala and French have the lion's share, Lingala scores more than French. The three other national languages are mentioned where Kikongo and Ciluba have more scores than Kiswahili.

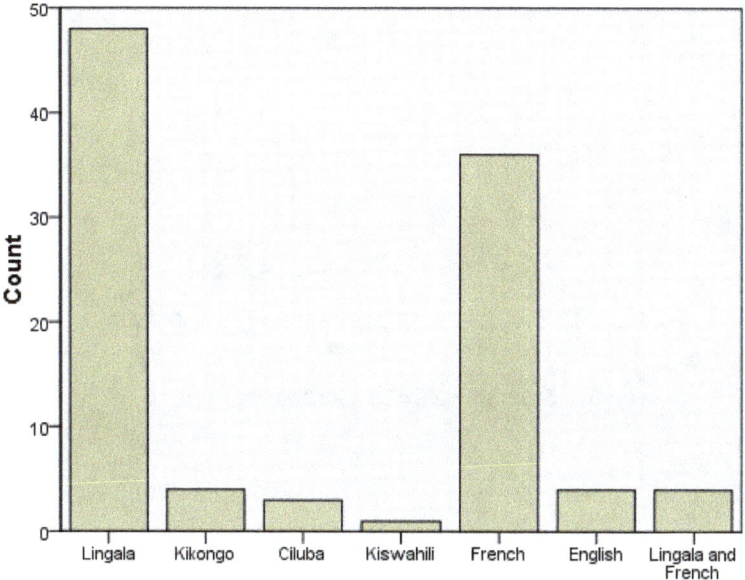

Figure 4: languages used in a quarrel

It is a surprise to notice that English is also mentioned by a few participants. This shows that there are a few participants who think it is still important to include English while using multilingual teaching as it can be seen in the figure above.

III.2.2.3 Languages of smooth expression

French has scored the highest of all the languages. Lingala has scored less and other national languages such as Ciluba and Kiswahili. None of the respondents mentioned Kikongo and a few respondents pointed English language. The figure below shows it:

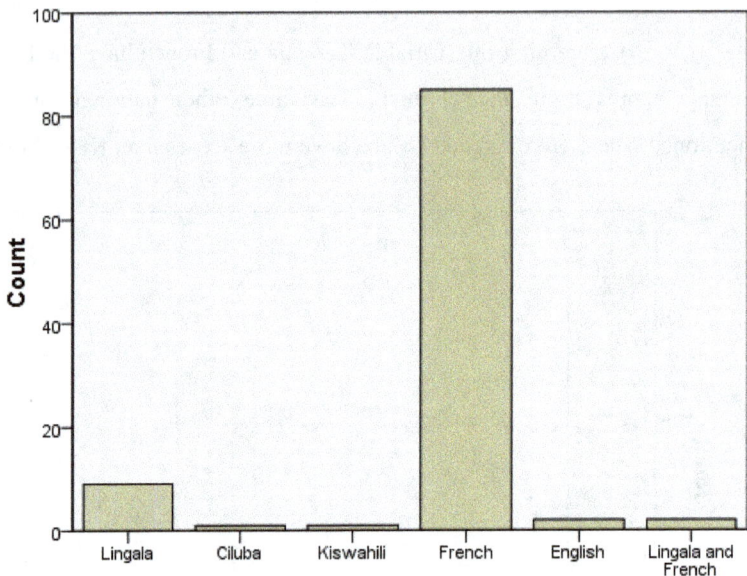

Figure 5: languages of smooth expression

III.2.2.4 Languages used in trouble

In trouble both French and Lingala are on the top. It is followed by the mixture of French and Lingala and Ciluba and Kiswahili are mentioned respectively two respondents. One of the respondents said he uses English while he is in trouble as illustrated in the following figure:

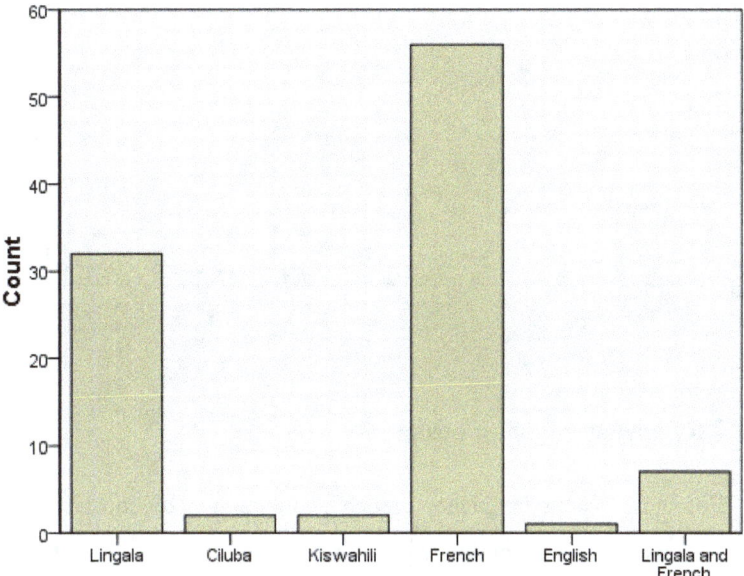

Figure 6. languages used in trouble

III.2.2.5 Languages of intimacy expression

For intimacy, the participants mentioned mostly French. Lingala is followed and Both Ciluba and English are mentioned by two participants. Eight participants have mentioned a mixture of French and Lingala as illustrated below:

Figure 7: languages of intimacy expression

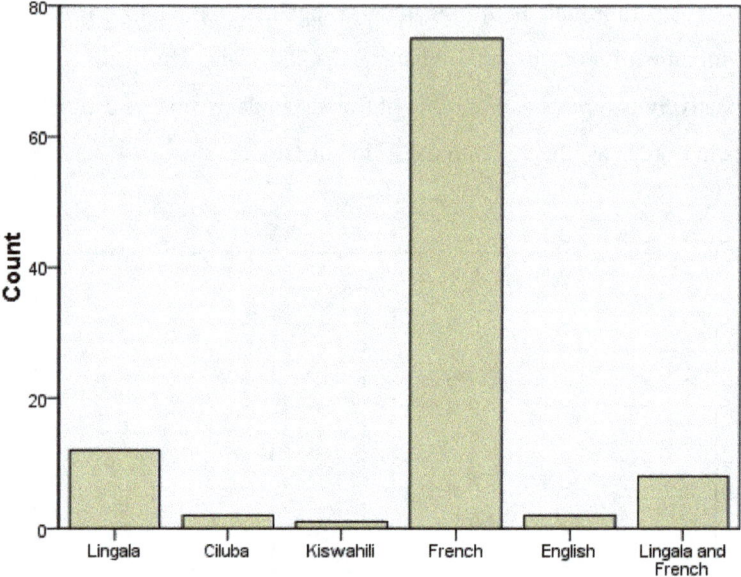

III.2.2.6 Languages of mass media

For mass media language, French is mentioned by most of the participants. English is also pointed by six respondents while one of the participants spoke in Ciluba, a national language. The following figure reveals it:

Figure 8: languages of mass media

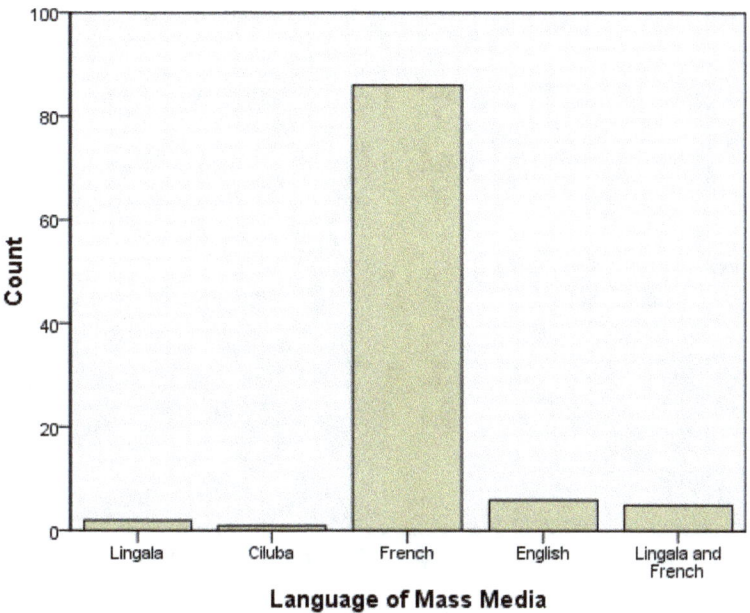

III.2.2.7 Languages of confided in writing

For this parameter, French is mostly mentioned by the participants. Lingala, Ciluba and Kikongo are also pointed by a few respondents. One participant says English is the language he confides in writing. The following figure reveals it:

Figure 9: languages of confided in writing

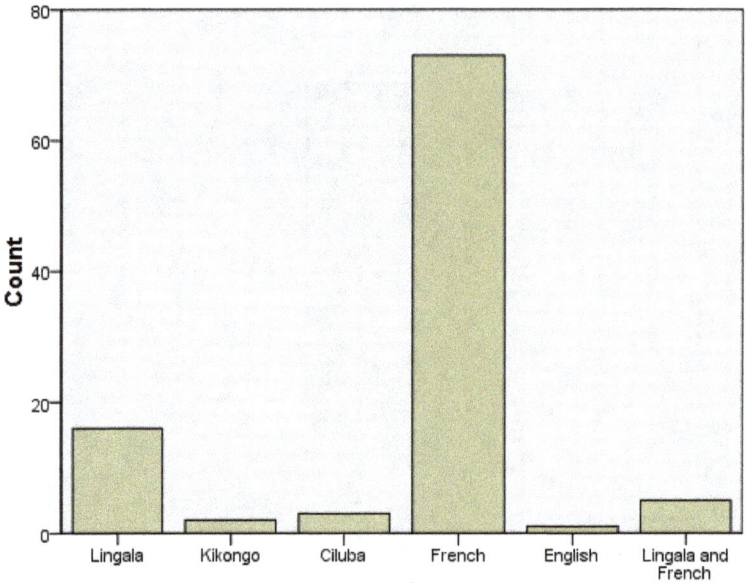

III.2.2.7 Languages of confided in reading

The results concerning this variable is similar to the preceding one, French also scores the highest. However, Lingala scores less and two participants mentioned English. The following figure shows it:

Figure 10: languages of confided in reading

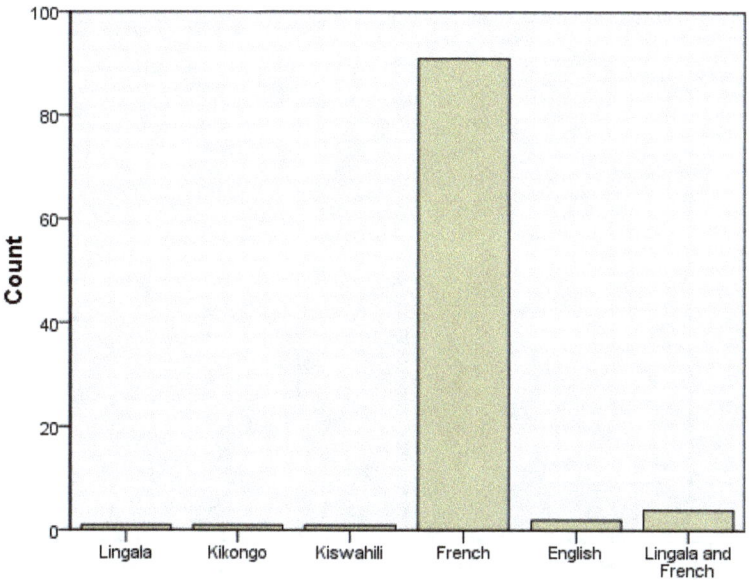

III.2.2.8 Languages of easy understanding

For easy understanding, French scores the most. Lingala is mentioned by some respondents while a few of them pointed Kikongo, Ciluba, a mixture of French and Lingala and English as shown below:

Figure 11: languages of easy understanding

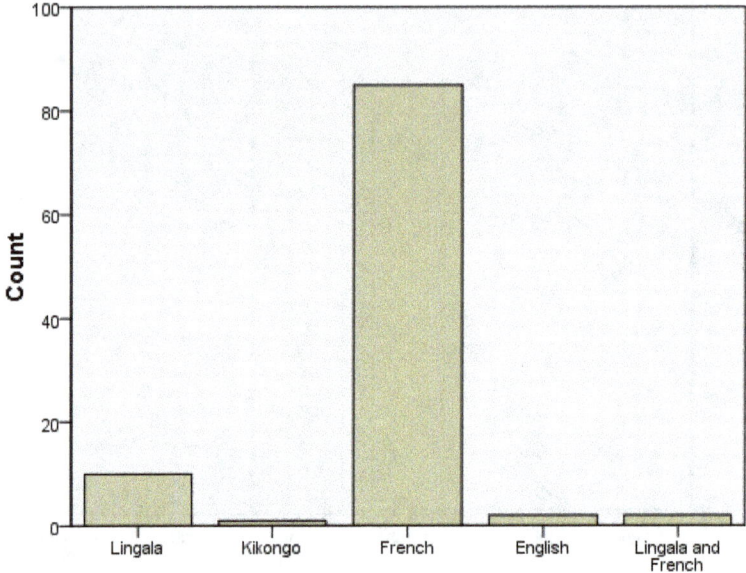

III.2.2.9 Languages preferred to follow classes

To follow classes, most of the participants prefer French which has the highest scores. Lingala is preferred by some participants and two participants prefer English. The figure shows the situation overtly:

Figure 12: languages preferred to follow classes

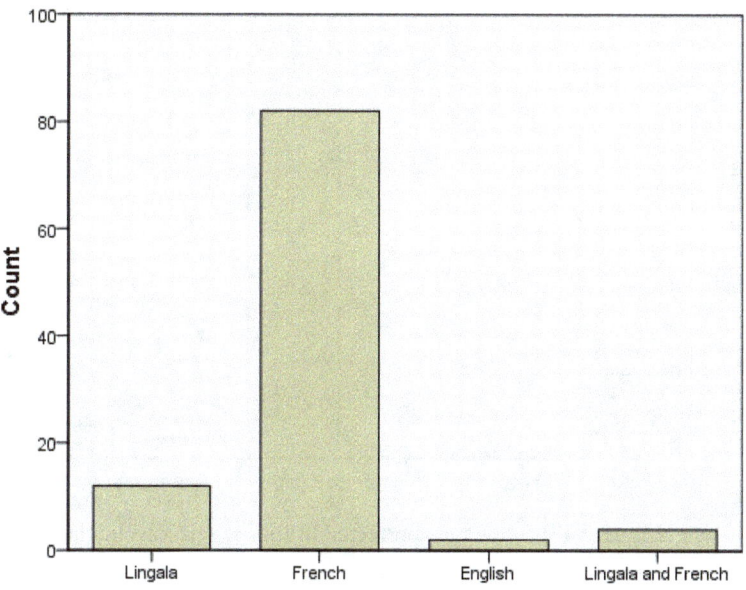

III.2.2.10 Languages preferred to follow sermons in church

For sermons, French is also mostly mentioned by the participants. Some participants pointed Lingala and a few mentioned Kikongo, Ciluba and English, the latter is pointed three respondents as indicated in the figure below:

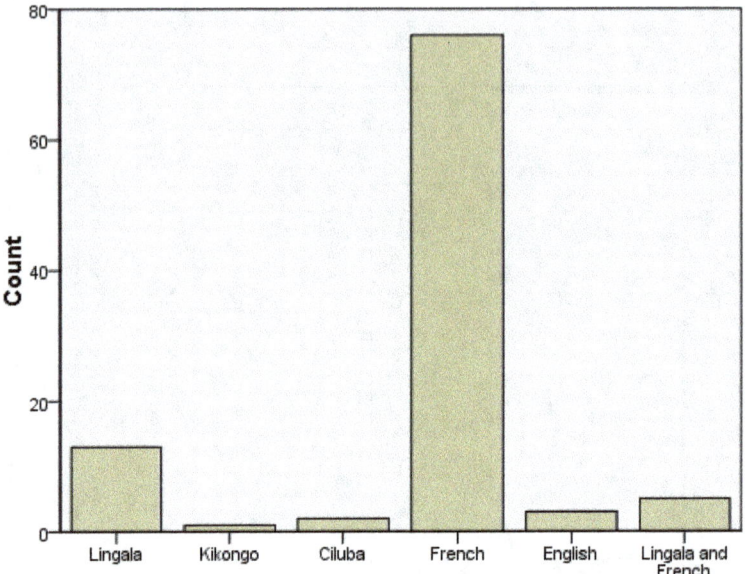

Figure: 13: languages preferred to follow sermons in church

III.2.2.11 Languages preferred to follow english classes

French is the languages preferred to follow English classes. A few of the participants mentioned a mixture of Lingala and French. One of the participants pointed Lingala and eight of them prefer English. The following figure shows the situation:

Figure 14: languages preferred to follow English classes

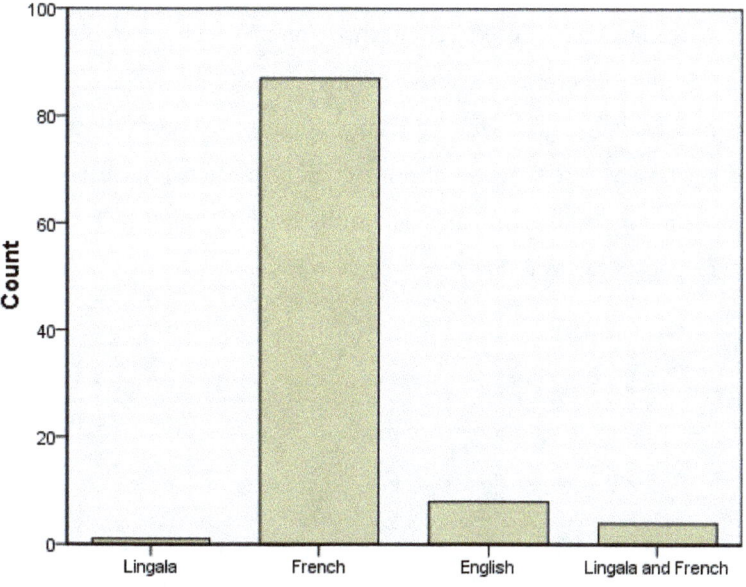

III.2.2.12 Views of the respondents concerning multilingualism in teaching English

Reading the listed comments, among the sixty-four participants of those who provided answers only three of them are against integrating other languages while teaching English. Almost all the participants who answered are for the Integration of Both French and English or a mixture of the two languages while teaching English. Their individual responses run as follows:

Table n° 0: Views of the participants concerning multilingualism in teaching English

Views of the participants concerning multilingualism in teaching English

Valid	Frequency	Percent	Valid Percent	Cumulative Percent
Not provided	38	38,0	38,0	38,0
An English teacher is supposed to be multicultural, apart from integrating the learners' languages, he can also refer to his or her culture for the best understanding	1	1,0	1,0	39,0
English is difficult, it is better to integrate French and Lingala while learning it	3	3,0	3,0	42,0
French allows us to better understand English class	1	1,0	1,0	43,0
French and Lingala are important while learning English	1	1,0	1,0	44,0
French and Lingala while learning English are helpful,	1	1,0	1,0	45,0
French and Lingala while learning English is helpful,	4	4,0	4,0	49,0
French is necessary While learning English	4	4,0	4,0	53,0
French while Learning English is helpful,	11	11,0	11,0	64,0
I am against the use of other languages while teaching English	1	1,0	1,0	65,0
I do not think integrating other languages is important	1	1,0	1,0	66,0
I prefer a teacher to teach English	1	1,0	1,0	67,0

III. 3 Interview data analysis

This third section is also subdivided into two subsections. The first one presents the interview data identification variables and the second one deals with the interview research interest variables.

III.3.1 Interview data identification variables

Two variables were used for identification variable in the interview.

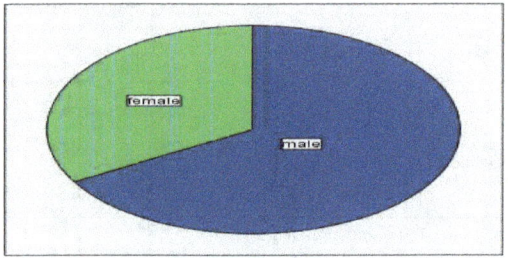

They are namely, gender and age.

III.3.1.1 Gender

After analyzing the results of the interview, it is disclosed that female students dominate over male students. The proportions of male students representing (66.7%) and the double of these proportions are female students as illustrated in the pie chart below:

Here, male students dominate female students. This can also be explained in the sense that male students were more available for the scheduled interview than female students.

III.3.1.2 Age

The results reveal the age group ranging from 18 to 25 at the top with (60%).

The remaining age group scores less.

III.3 .2 Interview data research interest variables

III.3.2.1 Languages expressed in a court

For this variable, the fifteen respondents who were selected to participate in the interview went straightforward by mentioning French. All of them selected French as the language expressed in a court.

Languages used in a court

Valid	Frequency	Percent	Valid Percent	Cumulative Percent
French	15	100,0	100,0	100,0

III.3.2.2 Languages used in a quarrel

The result on languages expressed in a quarrel is inclusive; all the participants mentioned a mixture of Lingala and French.

Languages expressed in a quarrel

Valid	Frequency	Percent	Valid Percent	Cumulative Percent
Lingala and French	15	100,0	100,0	100,0

III.3.2.3 Languages of smooth expression

The same situation is reported for language of smooth expression, Lingala and French are mentioned by all of them.

Languages of smooth expression

Valid	Frequency	Percent	Valid Percent	Cumulative Percent
Lingala and French	15	100,0	100,0	100,0

III.3.2.4. Languages expressed in trouble

For languages expressed in trouble, it is interesting to notice that there are different language strings. The string made of the mixture of Lingala and French scores the most and the remaining four participants who expressed verbally mentioned different languages. They also pointed Lingala, French and Kikongo. One of the participants mentioned other languages which could one of the vernacular languages.

Languages expressed in trouble

Valid	Frequency	Percent	Valid Percent	Cumulative Percent
Lingala and French	11	73,3	73,3	73,3
Lingala, Kikongo and French	1	6,7	6,7	80,0
Lingala, Kikongo and English	1	6,7	6,7	86,7
Lingala, Kikongo and other languages	1	6,7	6,7	93,3
Lingala, Kiswahili and French	1	6,7	6,7	100,0
Total	15	100,0	100,0	

III.3.2.5. Languages of intimacy expression

For intimacy, all the interviewed participants pointed Lingala and French.

Languages of intimacy expression

Valid	Frequency	Percent	Valid Percent	Cumulative Percent
Lingala and French	15	100,0	100,0	100,0

III.3.2.6. Languages of mass media

Responses from the interviewees reveal mostly French. One of them mentioned a string made of French and English.

Language of Mass Media

Valid	Frequency	Percent	Valid Percent	Cumulative Percent
French	14	93,3	93,3	93,3
French and English	1	6,7	6,7	100,0
Total	15	100,0	100,0	

III.3.2.7. Languages confided in writing

Looking at the tabulated result, French is mentioned by all the interviewees. It occurs in different strings with Lingala, Lingala and Kikongo and with English.

Languages confided in writing

Valid	Frequency	Percent	Valid Percent	Cumulative Percent
French	11	73,3	73,3	73,3
Lingala and French	1	6,7	6,7	80,0
French and English	2	13,3	13,3	93,3
Lingala, Kikongo and French	1	6,7	6,7	100,0
Total	15	100,0	100,0	

III.3.2.8. Languages confided in reading

In reading, it is not the same situation. Many of them mentioned Lingala and French. The latter is selected by the remaining participants where it is mixed with other languages as it is illustrated in the table below:

Languages confided in reading

Valid	Frequency	Percent	Valid Percent	Cumulative Percent
French	5	33,3	33,3	33,3
Lingala and French	8	53,3	53,3	86,7
Kiswahili and French	1	6,7	6,7	93,3
Lingala, Kikongo and French	1	6,7	6,7	100,0
Total	15	100,0	100,0	

III.3.2.9. Languages of easy understanding

For easy understanding, a mixture of Lingala and French are selected by the interviewees.

Languages of easy understanding

Valid	Frequency	Percent	Valid Percent	Cumulative Percent
Lingala and French	15	100,0	100,0	100,0

III.3.2.10. Languages of preference to follow classes

A mixture of Lingala and French are selected by all the interviewees.

They prefer the two languages to follow classes.

Languages of preference to follow classes

Valid	Frequency	Percent	Valid Percent	Cumulative Percent
Lingala and French	15	100,0	100,0	100,0

III.3.2.11. Languages of preference to attend religious sermons in church

All interviewees have opted for a combination of Lingala and French as their preferred languages to attend religious sermons.

Languages of preference to attend religious sermon in church

Valid	Frequency	Percent	Valid Percent	Cumulative Percent
French	8	53,3	53,3	53,3
Lingala and French	7	46,7	46,7	100,0
Total	15	100,0	100,0	

III.3.2.12. Languages of preference to follow english classes

To take English classes, you can choose either French or Lingala. In one option, only French is used, while in the other option, both French and Lingala are mixed together.

Languages of preference to follow English classes

Valid	Frequency	Percent	Valid Percent	Cumulative Percent
French	8	53,3	53,3	53,3
Lingala and French	7	46,7	46,7	100,0
Total	15	100,0	100,0	

III.3.2.13. Views of the participants concerning mutilingualism in teaching english

All the interviewees are for the integration of other languages while teaching English. There are those who mention French alone and others who mix it with Lingala.

Views of the participants concerning multilingualism in teaching English

Valid	Frequency	Percent	Valid Percent	Cumulative Percent
French is the language we understand best, it is easy to understand when a teacher uses it while teaching English	1	6,7	6,7	6,7
French and Lingala serve as understanding English	1	6,7	6,7	13,3
French and Lingala Facilitates understanding while learning English	1	6,7	6,7	20,0
French and Lingala serve as understanding English, a foreign language	3	20,0	20,0	40,0
French is the language we than other languages, use while learning English is advantageous	1	6,7	6,7	46,7
French serves as a bridge for understanding English	1	6,7	6,7	53,3

I prefer to translate some difficult words, but not to be taught English for example in Lingala	1	6,7	6,7	60,0
If a teacher has recourse to French while teaching, it hepls us understand best	1	6,7	6,7	66,7
Other languages are important while teaching or learning English, There are words which better expressed in our national languages,	2	13,3	13,3	80,0
Other languages as for examples Lingala and French are useful, mainly for beginners to better	1	6,7	6,7	86,7

III.4 The results of the monolingual and multilingual teaching tests

As mentioned early, after identifying the perfect mother tongues of the participants, the researcher wearing a cap of a sociolinguist recommended a teaching assistant to teach the participants who returned their written questionnaire copies. They were a hundred and all of them participated in the two English classes with the topic of reported speech. The choice of grammar lesson as the researcher found it interesting to test them within this micro competence. Another reason is thanks to accuracy of Grammar where flexibility in responses is reduced, looking like mathematics. The two tests were scores out of ten. The researcher participated in the correction, too. The following subsection focuses on Monolingual teaching test results.

III.4.1 Monolingual teaching test results

The monolingual teaching test results are the results obtained after teaching (the reported speech) basing on one language. Here, the teaching assistant, whatever methods he used which is less interesting for us, used only one language, English, the target language. After this teaching, the researcher submitted a test related to the items taught.

As one can observe, the participants secured six different scores out of ten as they are presented in increasing order. An important number of the participants failed with (1/10). Many of them secured 4/10 and 3/10. A few of them succeed with 5/10 and fewer secured 6/10.

The following table provides more clarification, mainly concerning the number of those failed and those who tried to succeed in out of a hundred participants:

Monolingual teaching test

Valid	Frequency	Percent	Valid Percent	Cumulative Percent
1	39	39,0	39,0	39,0
2	11	11,0	11,0	50,0
3	15	15,0	15,0	65,0
4	27	27,0	27,0	92,0
5	7	7,0	7,0	99,0
6	1	1,0	1,0	100,0
Total	100	100,0	100,0	

Observing the table, only a participant succeeded with 6/10 beyond the average scores. This implies the success of 1/100. Seven participants secured the average, if we consider the average as success, so 8/100 of success or 8% of success and 92% of failure.

III.4.2 Multilingual teaching test results

Taking into account the general tendency of the participants' perfect mother tongues, which is detailed the following chapter entitled interpretation and findings, the teaching assistant was recommended a second teaching where French and Lingala were integrated.

Here, the participants secured all the different scores as it is ordered from 1 to 10. A considerable proportion of the respondents secured 5,6 and4 out of ten. There are participants who secured the maxima of scores. It is interesting to discover that those succeeded scored from (5 to 10). The details on the number of those succeeded and failed are illustrated in the table below

Multilingual teaching Test				
Valid	Frequency	Percent	Valid Percent	Cumulative Percent
1	4	4,0	4,0	4,0
2	7	7,0	7,0	11,0
3	14	14,0	14,0	25,0
4	16	16,0	16,0	41,0
5	27	27,0	27,0	68,0
6	16	16,0	16,0	84,0
7	8	8,0	8,0	92,0
8	3	3,0	3,0	95,0
9	1	1,0	1,0	96,0
10	4	4,0	4,0	100,0
Total	100	100,0	100,0	

If we consider average as success, it can be observed that fifty-nine participants succeeded in. This implies the success of (59%). The sheets of the ten participants who failed in the monolingual test and succeeded in the multilingual one are attached as appendix.

III. 5. Interpretation

In this section, both the results of the survey questionnaire and interview are triangulated following the feature of mixed methods. For the sake clarity, tabulation is applied while the two results are corroborated:

III. 5.1 Gender

After corroborating the results of gender in both survey questionnaire and interview, the following can be observed:

Table N°4   Gender of the participants triangulated

	Survey questionnaire		Interview	
Valid	**Frequency**	**Percent**	**Frequency**	**Percent**
Male	37	37.0	10	66.7
Female	63	63.0	5	33.7
Total	100	100.0	15	100.0

The interview is dominated by males, whereas female students constitute the dominant groups in the survey questionnaire. As already mentioned, the researcher invited few students to an interview in a café which means out of 250 students in total, 25 have been selected representing one tenth. The choice of this setting can be explained by the fact that the researcher wanted to enjoy the comfort of a café, which also had psychological significance. The same ten questions of research interest were used in the interview; they were all open-ended.

The researcher estimated the age of the participants since gender did not have to be asked. All ten questions are shown in Appendix B.

The test

In this dissertation, classical test theory was applied. This theory is about test scores which introduces three concepts (1) test score (2) true score and (3) error score (Hambleton and Jones, 1993).

Vincent and Shammugan (2020) mention that the test score also denotes the observed test scores for each individual person the result of the actual ability of the examinee, which is influenced by errors, is either higher or lower. For the sake of a simple quantification of marks, researchers were not interested in the four basic language skills, but in micro-skills, which are grammar, vocabulary, pronunciation and spelling (Aydogan and Akbarov, 2014).

The university is located in an urban environment, specifically in the municipality of Lemba. The reason for the choice is simple: the researcher wanted to conduct the survey in a location where expertise would be readily available. Data Production/Collection In order to collect reliable data, it is important for the researcher to identify the source from which the data will be collected and then to know the procedures and tools that will be used to collect the data required for the study should.

Data can be collected from many sources including written documents, records, workplaces, the internet, surveys or interviews (Cohen, 2011).

Video recordings and observations are initially used to collect data. Questionnaires and semi-structured interviews are then used, but only with one group of the 25 people who were available — the others simply refused to participate and not force them to take part. In order to give examples of translanguaging and to find out the reality of local language use, all activities that took place outside the lecture hall during class were recorded.

It was a surprise to see a lecturer giving a philosophy class by explaining complex concepts to students in Lingala, the local language, or doing homework or classwork even though the students did not seem to understand anything. This is the lesson taught on direct and indirect speech in English translated into French and Lingala.

III.5.2 Age

After corroborating the results of age in both survey and interview, the following can be observed:

Table N°5   Age of the participants triangulated

Valid	Survey questionnaire		Interview	
	Frequency	Percent	Frequency	Percent
18 to 25	96	96.0	11	59.7
26 to 29	4	4.0	4	40.3
30 +				
Total	100	100.0	15	100.0

In both survey and interview, young students dominate. The age group of 26 to 29 has the similar proportion in both survey and interview. It shows a true convergence.

III.5.3 Languages expressed in a court

After corroborating the results of languages expressed in a court in both survey and interview, the following can be observed:

Table N°6. Languages expressed in a court of the participants triangulated

Valid	Survey questionnaire		Interview	
	Frequency	Percent	Frequency	Percent
Lingala	19	19.0		
Lingala and French	2	2.0		
Kiswahili	1	1.0		
French	77	77.0	100	100.0
English	1	1.0		
Total	100	100.0	100	100.0

The similar results on language choice are only noticed at the level of French. The survey provided a variety of language where French is also mentioned in mixture with Lingala. Kiswahili is mentioned by a participant in the survey. This is not against the Congolese constitution where any Congolese can use the language, he or she understands the best. The other participant who mentioned English might have not selected it.

III.5.4 Languages used in a quarrel

After checking the results of languages used in a quarrel in both survey questionnaire and interview, we can make the following observation:

Table N°7: Languages used in a quarrel of the participants

Valid	Survey questionnaire		Interview	
	Frequency	Percent	Frequency	Percent
Lingala	48	48.0		
Kikongo	4	4.0		
Ciluba	3	3.0		
Kiswahili	1	1.0		1
French	36	36.0	100	100.0
English	4	4.0		
Lingala and French	4	4.0		
Total	100	100.0	100	100.0

The survey questionnaire and interviews conducted in French revealed interesting results. The survey questionnaire included all four national languages, with Lingala scoring higher than the other national languages. According to the University police office, students tend to express themselves in Lingala during conflicts. It is possible that students who mentioned English did not actually use it.

III. .5. 5 Languages of smooth expression

After checking the results of languages of smooth expression in both survey and interview, we can make the following observation:

Table N°8 Languages of smooth expression of the participants triangulated

Valid	Survey questionnaire		Interview	
	Frequency	Percent	Frequency	Percent
Lingala	9	9.0		
Ciluba	1	1.0		
Kiswahili	1	1.0		
French	85	85.0	15	100.0
English	2	2.0		
Lingala and French	2	2.0		
Total	100	100.0	15	100.0

Here, the surveyed students mostly selected French and all the interviewees selected it, too. The national languages are mentioned, but Lingala itself and mixed with French is also selected. This shows the strength of Lingala after French.

III..5. 6. Languages used in trouble

After checking the results of languages used in trouble in both survey questionnaire and interview, we can make the following observation:

Table N°9 Languages used in trouble of the participants triangulated

Valid	Survey questionnaire		Interview	
	Frequency	Percent	Frequency	Percent
Lingala	12	12.0		
Ciluba	2	2.0		
Kiswahili	1	1.0		
Lingala, Kikongo			3	20.0
Lingala, Kiswahili and French			1	
French	75	75.0		
English	2	2.0		
Lingala and French	8	8.0	11	73.0
Total	100	100.0	15	100.0

The survey mentions French with the highest scores while the interview shows the mixture of French and Lingala with the highest scores, too. Other national languages including English are selected in the survey. No one of the interviewees mentioned English as a language expresses in trouble.

III. .5. 7 Languages of intimacy

After corroborating the results of languages of intimacy in both survey questionnaire and interview, the following can be observed:

Table N°10 Languages of intimacy of the participants triangulated

	Survey questionnaire		Interview	
Valid	**Frequency**	**Percent**	**Frequency**	**Percent**
Lingala	12	12.0		
Ciluba	2	2.0		
Kiswahili	1	1.0		
Lingala and French	8	8.0	15	100.0
French	75	75.0		
English	2	2.0		
Total	100	100.0	15	100.0

The variety of languages is selected by the participants in the survey questionnaire. The interview is stuck to the mixture of French and Lingala. Lingala shows its strength as it is mentioned itself by some surveyed participants.

III..5. 8 Languages of mass media

After corroborating the results of languages of mass media n both survey and interview, the following can be observed:

Table N°11 Languages of mass media of the participants triangulated

	Survey questionnaire		Interview	
Valid	**Frequency**	**Percent**	**Frequency**	**Percent**
Lingala	2	2.0		
Ciluba	1	1.0		
French	86	86.0	15	100.0
Lingala and French	5	5.0		
English	6	6.0		
Total	100	100.0	15	100.0

The results do not deny French in both survey questionnaire and interview. All the interviewees select it, too. English as the language of the mass media is recognized by a few surveyed participants.

III.5.9 Languages confided in writing

After corroborating the results of languages confided in writing in both survey questionnaire and interview, the following can be observed:

Table N°12 Languages confided in writing of the participants triangulated

Valid	Survey questionnaire		Interview	
	Frequency	Percent	Frequency	Percent
Lingala	16	16.0		
Ciluba	3	3.0		
French	73	73.0	11	73.0
French and English			2	13.3
Lingala and French	5	5.0	1	6.7
Kikongo	2	2.0		
Lingala, Kikongo and French			1	6.7
English	1	1.0		
Total	100	100.0	15	100.0

III. .5. 10 Languages confided in reading

After corroborating the results of languages confided in reading in both survey and interview, the following can be observed:

Table N°13 Languages confided in reading of the participants triangulated

	Survey questionnaire		Interview	
Valid	Frequency	Percent	Frequency	Percent
Lingala	1	1.0		
French	91	91.0	5	33.3
Kiswahili and French			1	6.7
Lingala and French	5	5.0	8	53.3
Kikongo	2	2.0		
Lingala, Kikongo and French			1	6.7
English	2	2.0		
Total	100	100.0	15	100.0

The results show the variety of languages in both survey questionnaire and interview. Looking at the languages selected both sides. French and Lingala and French dominate. Other languages are mentioned. There is a doubt for the two respondents in the survey who selected English that I think has not yet become the language they confide in reading.

III.5.11 Languages of easy understanding

After confirming results of languages in both survey and interview that are easy to understand we can see the following:

Table N°14: Languages of easy understanding of the participants triangulated

	Survey questionnaire		Interview	
Valid	Frequency	Percent	Frequency	Percent
Lingala	10	10.0		
Kikongo	1	1.0		
French	85	85.0		
Lingala and French	2	2.0	15	100.0
English	2	2.0		
Total	100	100.0	15	100.0

It is revealed that in both survey and interview, French, Lingala and French and Lingala itself are the dominant ones. Other languages including English are mentioned.

III.5.12 Languages of preference to follow classes

After corroborating the results of languages preferred to follow classes in both survey and interview, the following can be observed:

Table N°15. Languages of preference to follow classes of the participants triangulated

	Survey questionnaire		Interview	
Valid	**Frequency**	**Percent**	**Frequency**	**Percent**
Lingala	12	12.0		
French	82	82.0		
Lingala and French	4	4.0	15	100.0
English	2	2.0		
Total	100	100.0	15	100.0

To follow classes in general, the participants of the interview have all mixed Lingala and French. French is mentioned in the survey, too.

III.5. 13 Languages of preference to follow sermon in church

After corroborating the results of languages preferred to follow sermon in church in both survey and interview, the following can be observed:

Table N°16 Languages of preference to follow sermon in the church of the participants triangulated

	Survey questionnaire		Interview	
Valid	**Frequency**	**Percent**	**Frequency**	**Percent**
Lingala	13	12.0		
Kikongo	1	1.0		
Ciluba	2	2.0		
French	76	76.0	8	53.3
Lingala and French	5	5.0	7	46.7
English	3	3.0		
Total	100	100.0	15	100.0

As it is recognized, one follows sermon to understand it. In both survey and interview, French and Lingala are mentioned. Lingala is also mixed with French.

III.5.14 Languages of preference to follow English classes

After corroborating the results of languages of preference to follow English classes in both survey questionnaire and interview, the following can be observed:

Table N°17 Languages of preference to follow English classes of the participants triangulate

	Survey questionnaire		Interview	
Valid	Frequency	Percent	Frequency	Percent
Lingala	1	1.0		
French	87	87.0	8	53.3
Lingala and French	4	5.0	7	46.7
English	8	8.0		
Total	100	100.0	15	100.0

To follow English classes, in both survey questionnaire and interview, the participants mentioned mostly both French and Lingala. The two languages show convergence in both survey and interview are French and French mixed with Lingala. The two languages are mentioned by the study participants to be the languages of preference to follow English classes. This can be systematically established in the study with the procedure applied by Nsimambote (2023).

III.5.15 Views of the participants concerning multilingualism in teaching triangulated

To restrict to important groups of participants who provided views on both survey and interview, the following table exhibits:

Table N°18 Views of the participants triangulated

Views	Survey questionnaire		Interview	
	Frequency	Percent	Frequency	Percent
French and Lingala while learning English is helpful,	15	15.0		
French is necessary while learning English	4	4.0		
French and Lingala serve as a bridge for understanding English, a foreign language			3	20.0
Other languages are important while teaching or learning English, There are words which better expressed in our national languages,			2	13.3

In the survey questionnaire, the important groups consisted of respectively of 15 and 4 students who all mention French, but the one of 15 students mixed it with Lingala as the 3 students in the survey. The other interviewed group of 2 students extended Lingala to other languages. Sure, in the context of Kinshasa, it is difficult to require a lecture to extend his multilingualism to the learners' languages. A lecture is not able for examples to have a good command of mother tongues of his learners.

III. 6. FINDINGS

Among the research objectives targeted in this dissertation the following, namely establishing the participants' multilingualism by identifying their perfect mother and the one of find out the difference in performance between learners taught in monolingual and multilingual teaching.

To cope with the above-mentioned objectives, the establishment of the respondents' multilingualism by identifying the respondents' perfect mother tongues has the following findings.

III. 6 .1 Identifying the participants' perfect mother tongues

Both the survey questionnaire data and interview ones were needed to identify the perfect mother tongues whose knowledge was important to move to tests. In the survey questionnaire, the following table provides illustration on the perfect mother tongues basing on Nsimambote's procedure (2023) was applied in the table below:

Table N°18:   Perfect mother tongues establishment (Survey)

The table below provided shows the perfect mother tongues of the students we surveyed taking into account the socio psychological parameters that have been established.

Our analysis indicates that for some learners Lingala is the perfect (dominant) mother tongue while for others French has a significant influence. This conclusion was drawn from the data gathered through our survey questions and interviews which can be found in the appendix at the end of this work.

LANGUAGES OF THE SPEAKER	SOCIO-PSYCHOLINGUISTIC PARAMETERS	RELATED SKILLS	VARIABLES	FRENCH
EASIER LANGUAGES OF THE SPEAKER	LANGUAGES OF EMOTIONAL EXPRESSION	SPEAKING	Languages expressed in a court	77
			Languages expressed in quarrel	36
			Languages of smooth expression	85
		READ SPEAKING	Languages expressed in trouble	56
			Languages of intimacy expression	75
		READING	Languages confided in reading	91
		WRITING	Languages confided in writing	73
		LISTENING	Languages of easy understanding	85
			Languages preferred To follow classes	82
			Languages preferred To follow sermon in church	76
			Languages preferred To follow English classes	87
			Languages of mass (var9)	86
Total				909

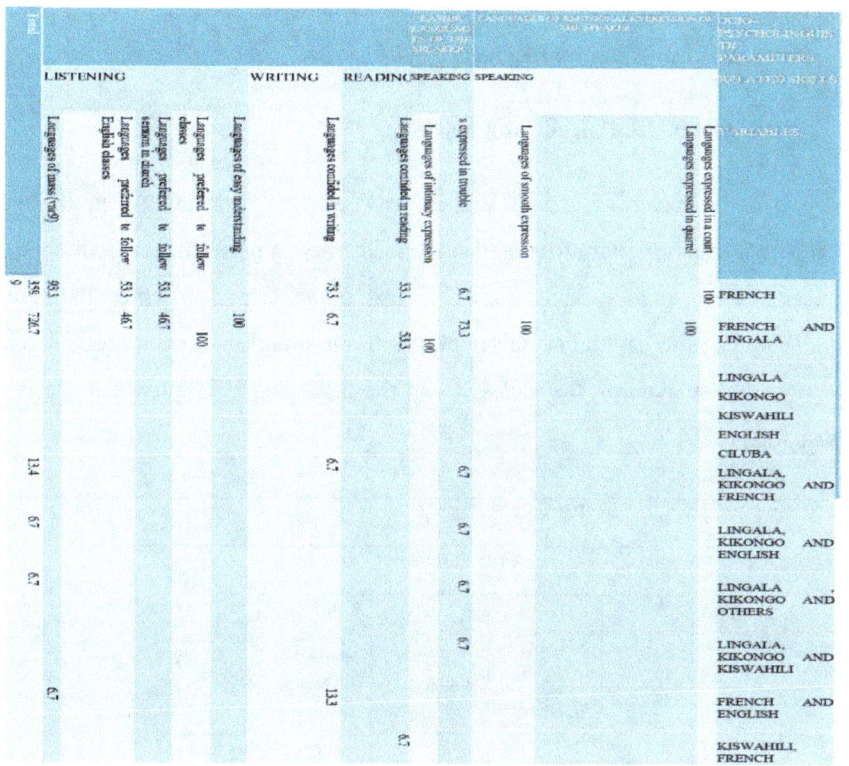

In the survey, total of language string reveal with the proportions of 990. It is followed by Lingala itself with 175. In the interview, French and Lingala have the highest proportions with 726.7. It is followed by French with

359.9. With the light of the above French and Lingala, either singly or mixed emerge as the perfect mother of the participants. As the study was sequential, these findings of both survey and interview enlightened the researcher to select no other languages but French and Lingala in the multilingual teaching to demonstrate their impact on the teaching and learning of English language.

III.6. 2. Difference in performance between learners taught through mono and multilingual teaching

Table N°19. Paired samples test

Concerning the difference between monolingual and multilingual teaching it was important to establish the difference in performance to do this, we had used t-test, mainly paired sampled t-test as the score secured by the similar students that is to say the same sample. Both the multilingual and monolingual t scores are displayed on the tables X and the following table provides clarity on the paired t-test.

		Paired samples test							
		Paired differences							
			Standard deviation	Mean standard Error	Confidence interval of the difference at 95%				Sig. (bilateral)
		Average			lower	higher			
Pair 1	MONOLINGUAL - MULTILINGUAL	-2,290	,935	,094	-2,476	-2,104	-24,486	99	,000

As it is illustrated in the above table. The difference between these two means is -2.290 ± 0.935, demonstrating the superiority of the multilingual approach over the monolingual method (t = -24.486; ddl = 99 and p<0.001). The multilingual approach is undoubtedly the most suitable method for teaching English to multilingual students. The test results have unequivocally proven this fact.

CHAPTER FOUR: RECOMMENDATIONS

The last objective of this dissertation talks about suggesting the multilingual approach in teaching English in order to help out in EFL classrooms. This is the focus of the current chapter. In the first section, a summary on approaches in teaching English including the multilingual one is provided and the second one emphasizes suggestions on the use the multilingual approach basing on the positive impact demonstrated in the current dissertation.

IV.1. Approaches in EFL

In this section, various approaches and methods in language teaching, including the multilingual one, are shown.

Different approaches and methods in language teaching have changed over time and may not always meet the needs of everyone.

Each individual has unique strengths, weaknesses, and learning preferences. Historically, in 1963, American linguist Edward Anthony categorized three levels of conceptualization and organization as approach, method, and technique.

An approach is a set of general principles about how language should be taught and learned. One important principle is that it explains the topic.

A method is an overall plan for how to teach language systematically, with each method being different and based on the chosen approach.

There are many methods, and a technique is something that is used in the classroom. Techniques must be connected to the method and match the process. Techniques are specific ways or strategies used to reach a short-term goal. There are different ways to teach, with some methods including the traditional method of teaching English in the 1800s called the grammar translation method (GTM).

This method was commonly used but prevented students from becoming fluent in spoken English. As a result, the GTM was criticized for being uncommunicative, boring, irrelevant, and unnecessary.

In simpler terms, it did not help students improve their ability to communicate effectively in the language. (Brown, 2002)

GTM is a language learning approach that is based on traditional Latin teaching methods like translating sentences from the first language into the new language and memorizing grammar rules and vocabulary words. It was first introduced in the early 19th century and is still used today.

The main focus is on writing and reading, with less emphasis on speaking and listening skills. Proponents of GTM argue that comprehending the language itself is essential to fully understand its grammar rules. Vocabulary is acquired to support grammar and then reinforced through translation exercises or grammar drills. Gouin (1880) was the first to develop this language learning technique by taking cues from how children naturally learn their first language.

The direct method, as advocated by L. Sauveur, was seen as a more authentic way of teaching, emphasizing the use of the target language and providing real-life examples. Other experts have also discussed the principles of the direct method.

According to Larsen Freeman and Anderson (2011), instructors using this method aim to enhance students' speaking skills in the target language with a strong focus on spoken communication.

Caleb Gattegno, in 1972, stressed the importance of students learning independently and highlighted the role of teachers as facilitators who should stay quiet during lessons.

According to Richards and Rodgers (2010), the main objective of the silent approach is to teach new language learners the basics of the target language through speaking and listening.

The focus is on developing conversation skills and expanding vocabulary before moving on to more complex skills like reading, listening, writing, and grammar in a structured way.

Brooks (1964) states that we usually learn to speak before we learn to read and write. It is commonly believed that our native language is spoken first, while written language is seen as a secondary skill.

Therefore, traditional language teaching has prioritized improving speaking skills first, with writing skills introduced later once a strong foundation has been set. However, solely relying on repetition and practice may only help beginners reach a basic level of proficiency, making it difficult to achieve higher levels of skill using this method.

In 1967, C.J. Dodson suggested a bilingual approach to teaching English along with other subjects. This method involves using the learner's first language to help them learn a new language. It focuses on comparing and contrasting the two languages, including intonation, vocabulary, and structure.

The main aim of the bilingual strategy is to improve the learning of a new language. When educators and learners recognize these distinctions, it becomes simpler for learners to understand the language.

Being familiar with situations they are accustomed to in their native language assists learners in comprehending the new language correctly and completely.

Total Physical Response (TPR) is a language learning strategy that integrates spoken language with physical movements. In this method, students act as both the audience and the participants, following their instructor's directions and acting out the movements. Krashen believes that TPR positions the instructor at the heart of the learning journey, where the teacher is actively engaged in guiding the students, monitoring their use of vocabulary, assessing their speaking progress, and offering feedback.

The structural approach to language learning sees language as a collection of grammatical patterns that need to be learned in a specific sequence. Rather than just memorizing words, this strategy emphasizes learning one grammatical pattern at a time, slowly building up abilities. This is similar to the way children naturally learn language.

For instance, the present continuous tense includes the use of "to be" as an auxiliary verb. This method can be applied in different language teaching approaches.

Structural techniques concentrate on instructing four fundamental language abilities: listening, speaking, reading, and writing (Ferdinand de Saussure, 1915).

The naturalistic strategy stresses the significance of input, stressing that students should perfect the pronunciation of new words before trying to articulate them.

Listening and reading are the primary focus of this approach, while speaking abilities improve gradually through exposure to real materials.

Thornbury (2006) suggests that teaching language should focus on actions and speaking before writing, rather than using translations and grammar explanations. Terrell (1977) believes that understanding vocabulary is more important than grammar in successful language learning.

Initially, teachers lead students in their learning, but as students become more proficient, they become more actively involved in their education. Richards (2010) states that the Natural approach emphasizes fluency and accuracy in producing sentences in the target language.

According to cognitive theory, individuals need to understand a concept before they can effectively express it in language, which applies to both first and second language acquisition.

Swiss psychologist Jean Piaget's theory from the 1930s highlights the importance of interacting with the world for mental development, which helps in language acquisition by improving cognitive skills like thinking, reading, learning, memory, reasoning, and attention.

The Communicative approach aims to help students develop good communication skills by focusing on all four language skills equally. Known as Communicative Language Instruction (CLI), this method encourages students to learn independently with little teacher involvement.

Teachers mainly help students when needed, like guiding them to find solutions if they can't resolve a misunderstanding after repeated attempts. While using the target language is preferred, students can also use their native language, especially for explaining grammar or translating complex ideas. CLI has become popular in Foreign Language education because it allows students to use their language skills in real-life situations outside of the classroom.

J. Gumperz and D. Hymes created communicative theories that suggest learning happens when people interact with each other, like teachers and students or students with each other. These theories emphasize how information is shared during these interactions, with the sender, message, and receiver being important including speaking, listening, reading, and writing is key in this approach. Today, many people still support the communicative approach using different techniques.

Holliday (1994) also suggests that students can work together in pairs or groups and do not have to speak only English; they can talk in their native language while doing communicative activities and making language assumptions.

Many theories have explored different parts of language learning such as how learners learn, their personal traits, and cultural impacts. Using these methods has helped us understand how effective they are in today's education system.

Most students are happy with better test results. College students often struggle with learning a new language that they haven't used before in their studies. Strategies like using dictionaries and translation tools have been added to teaching to help students learn better.

Even though some were unsure at first, these methods have been very effective, especially in countries where more than one language is spoken.

The idea of translanguaging has given better results, showing how important it is to embrace students' ability to speak multiple languages.

These methods have been crucial in helping students succeed in learning languages. Translanguaging, as explained by Otheguy et al. (2015), is a helpful teaching method that encourages teamwork between students and teachers, helping everyone in the class improve their language skills. This method goes beyond simple translation and focuses on making sure all students have the same opportunities to learn.

The main aim is to address language differences and make sure everyone's opinions are important. In college, translanguaging has been proven to change the way people communicate by giving a new outlook on education. Translanguaging is when people use more than one language at the same time to communicate effectively.

Bilingual and multilingual individuals use this approach to show that languages are connected and should be used together in certain situations. This idea was first introduced by Williams in 1996, who explained that it involves switching between languages during conversations. Garcia in 2014 further clarifies that translanguaging means using two or more languages simultaneously.

This concept helps individuals make use of all their language skills when communicating, offering a useful guide for language use. It is a helpful strategy for dealing with different interpretations and is used in both everyday conversations and academic settings for teaching purposes.

The concept of translanguaging is complex and can have different interpretations. Experts in linguistics have extensively debated about it, but the lack of a clear definition makes it hard to fully understand the concept.

Despite this, it is interesting to explore the various ways in which the term is used, starting with its origins.

Cen Williams, a Welsh scholar, first introduced the term in the 1980s in his work, the Welsh equivalent of "translanguaging," in an unpublished manuscript. Williams initially defined it narrowly, «focusing on using both English and Welsh in language teaching.

Translanguaging encourages EAL students to use all their language skills to help them succeed. This means they are encouraged to speak, write, and understand in both their native language and English to aid their learning.

Embracing translanguaging also involves promoting a positive view of being multilingual and boosting EAL students' pride in all their language skills. An important part of translanguaging is to allow students to choose which language they feel most comfortable using at any time. There are many ways to include translanguaging with EAL students, no matter their age or how well they speak English. Here are a few examples: "

1. Multilingual dictionaries are important tools that help ESL students improve their language skills by offering different meanings for familiar words.
2. Encouraging students to make a personalized list of important terms in both their native language and English can motivate them in class.

When tackling a challenging English assignment, such as writing an article for a magazine, ESL students often achieve better results by first writing in their native language and then translating it into English.

This method can help them communicate their ideas more effectively and create higher quality work. It is especially beneficial for students who are new to the English language or are still learning it. By following this approach, they can focus on their ideas without struggling to express them in English.

Later on, they can try translating it into English using a bilingual dictionary or translation tool. Online research allows students to decide if they want to conduct their studies in their native language or a mix of languages, like in a specific part of the DRC.

This is especially helpful for EAL learners who may prefer to use their mother tongue. Collaborative discussions on this platform give students the chance to talk with peers from different African countries who speak the same local languages, such as Congo Kinshasa and Brazzaville. These discussions can involve using English for EFL learners or Lingala for translanguaging purposes, where learners can freely choose which language to use. Translanguaging activities, like taking notes and discussing with peers who speak their first language, can help EAL learners get ready for exams in their first language if they are available. It is important to make students proud of their first language and give them access to texts that help with learning and understanding. Translanguaging is a useful approach for EAL learners because it lets them use their language and reading skills in their native language to improve their academic English skills.

By encouraging students to understand new ideas in their native language and then sharing that knowledge with English teachers, we can help them succeed. English teachers can effectively use their prior knowledge to enhance their teaching. Researchers like Garcia and Li support the use of translanguaging in the classroom to help EAL learners reach their full potential by utilizing their complete language skills.

Scholars and activists have long stressed the importance of promoting positive attitudes towards multilingualism. Skutnabb-Kangas introduced the idea of "linguistic human rights" to fight against linguistic discrimination, while Levy et al. highlighted the negative effects on learners whose native language is undervalued in educational settings.

Conteh also believes that incorporating multilingualism in schools can lead to academic success for EAL learners. The multilingual approach in teaching languages considers the diverse languages and cultures of students.

Using students' native language and cultural skills is encouraged when learning a new language, especially for those studying as a second or foreign language. Research has shown that learners often find their mother tongue to be a valuable asset in comprehension, as demonstrated through multilingual testing. Multilingualism, the ability to proficiently communicate in multiple languages like a native speaker, can enhance language learning and promote diversity in the classroom.

By incorporating multiple languages, students can leverage their existing language and cultural knowledge, as discussed in an article by Harshitha Jain. Recognizing and including students' diverse backgrounds can enrich language learning and understanding. Teachers play an important role in fostering this diversity and should encourage students to use their mother tongue as a resource in their language learning journey.

Using a multilingual approach to learn English is becoming more popular. This method involves encouraging learners to use both their native language and English as they work on improving their language skills. Educational experts refer to this as multilingual pedagogy.

By incorporating various languages in the classroom, students can better grasp the English language. It is crucial to remember that using different languages should support English learning, not replace it.

When you decide to use teaching methods, it is important to consider the students' preferences and learning needs. Being able to speak more than one language is a valuable skill that can help you in various aspects of life, such as connecting with others, appreciating different cultures, and improving cognitive abilities. The advantages of being multilingual are truly noticeable. Using their native language at home can assist learners in enhancing their English abilities, which has been shown to be beneficial for adults who are new to learning English. This approach can improve their comprehension and develop their confidence in speaking.

Adults who already know another language should use their past experiences and knowledge to help them learn a new language.

In the USA, there are many ways to learn English, and some countries even offer assistance to those wanting to improve their language skills.

They provide information in different languages to ensure everyone can understand. In Virginia, there are forms in various languages and videos to help with comprehension. In some States, high school tests can even be taken in languages other than English, such as Spanish.

By using this method, people can enhance their English skills more effectively. According to Galante (2019), using your own cultural and linguistic background as tools for literacy is a significant advantage.

It allows students to transfer their reading and writing skills from one language to another, making English their second, third, or even fourth language. In communities where many languages are spoken, it is common for teachers to encourage students to use their own language to help them learn.

Teachers believe that this is a useful tool and an important part of the classroom. This is different from programs that only focus on English and suggest that learning is best when using one's native language minimally. Contrary to what many people think, there is strong evidence that students who speak more than one language have sharper minds.

Developing cognitive abilities and cross-cultural communication skills are crucial for a student's academic success. In today's world, which is interconnected, it is important to increase our understanding of different cultures and languages.

By supporting multilingual education, we not only improve academic performance but also give students the tools they need to manage in our global society. According to Lo Bianco (2014), languages play a very important role in shaping educational environments.

Gogolin (2011) and Ellis (2011) stress that the value and significance placed on different languages in various countries, each reflecting its unique identity and abundant diversity.

While most people mainly speak their native language, many education systems offer instruction in multiple languages.

In Europe, English is commonly taught as a foreign language from an early age, showing its global importance.

The increasing popularity of Content and Language Integrated Learning (CLIL) programs shows a growing interest in improving students' proficiency in academic language. However, minority indigenous languages and immigrant dialects are often pushed aside and not given enough attention.

As mentioned by Ellis et al. (2011), this view is common in educational institutions and affects language teaching methods and curriculum decisions.The legacy of nineteenth-century efforts to standardize language still affects students who speak languages other than the dominant one in their region.

IV.2. Some recommendations

A suggestion put forth by Raoul Ekwampok is for the Congolese government to prioritize the promotion of linguistic patriotism and cultural development by actively encouraging the use of African languages. This entails the promotion and official recognition of national languages. Additionally, it is imperative to translate these languages into commonly spoken languages in various sectors such as education, law, media, administration, and business. Rather than treating them as mere subjects, these languages should be taught as a valuable tool for learning.

All citizens of the Democratic Republic of Congo should use Congolese languages competently to support national unity and good governance. To hold public leadership positions and strengthen national ties, educated Congolese must speak at least two of the country's national languages fluently. Schools should make bilingual education mandatory, and foreign languages should be emphasized in the curriculum, like in Tanzania. This method should be effective, reliable, and suited to the country's size and requirements.

It is essential to enact a new law that guarantees the allocation of resources required to support the four national languages. Furthermore, we must take the initiative to equip ourselves with the tools necessary for the promotion, commercialization, and preservation of Congolese culture.

The reestablishment of the Language Observatory is crucial for addressing the linguistic needs of the Congolese population in the face of ongoing Western imperialism and colonialism. The education system is struggling to create appropriate curricula and supply sufficient teaching resources, largely because of the wide variety of languages used throughout the nation.

It is crucial for students to receive instructions in a language that they are proficient in both speaking and comprehending. Investing in language at the university level is of utmost importance. Students should receive education in both their national tongue and a foreign language while their academic progress is closely monitored.

Integrating English into the curriculum alongside local languages offers significant benefits, provided that most students can effectively understand

and use it. Additionally, incorporating the national language at the university level enhances students' access to cultural insights. Education should be inclusive, honoring the linguistic and cultural backgrounds of all individuals. Importantly, this method does not require students to use the same ideas and language as their classmates in other countries.

Learning should take place in the language that the child is most familiar with promoting better understanding and learning outcomes. Making literature in the local language available to all community members, regardless of their circumstances, is essential.

Education in a specific area must be improved to ensure that everyone can access it, regardless of their location or financial situation. Freire (1970) emphasized that personalized learning is a powerful tool for empowering individuals and liberating them from restrictive educational practices. By integrating diverse resources and promoting linguistic variety, we can significantly improve the quality of life for everyone. Adopting these recommendations could enable the university to effectively tackle the challenges of fulfilling UNESCO's commitment to education in students' native languages. I wholeheartedly endorse the University of Kinshasa in spearheading this initiative, especially concerning the English language curriculum.

CONCLUSION

The current dissertation aims at demonstrating the positive impact of mother tongues on the learning of some students of media department of the University of Kinshasa. The topic is an innovative one since it deals with an approach using a multilingual approach or translanguaging method in teaching English to foreign learners. Three objectives were targeted:

To establish the perfect mother tongues of the participants.

To find out the difference in performance between students taught in mono and multilingual teaching

To suggest the multilingual approach or translanguaging method in teaching English in order to help out in EFL classrooms.

The assumptions below were the concern of the dissertation:

- Most of participants are perfect multilinguals in French and Lingala.
- There is a difference in performance between learners taught in monolingual teaching and those taught in multilingual one, which is demonstrated statistically.
- The multilingual teaching approach, which shows a positive impact, is appropriate for the concerned learners.

All of the three hypotheses were validated. Basing on both survey and interview, it was systematically established that the perfect mother tongues of the concerned are both French and Lingala as displayed on the table N0 and respectively entitled Perfect mother tongues establishment (survey) and Perfect mother tongues establishment (interview)

There is a difference in performance between learners taught in monolingual teaching and those taught in multilingual one. It is thanks to the positive impact of multilingual approach. The statistical demonstration exhibited the following:

The statistical hypotheses taken into account stated: If $M1 - M2 \geq 1$, there is a positive impact.

If $M1 - M2 \leq 0$, there is no impact or negative impact.

Applying the first statistical hypothesis stating that If $M1 - M2 \geq 1$, once applied, it yields.

4.84- 2.55= 2.29

Since 2.29 not ≤ 0, there is a positive impact.

This difference exhibited a positive impact of the use of multilingual approach in teaching English to the concerned students.

The third and last assumption stating that the multilingual teaching approach, which shows a positive impact, is appropriate for the concerned learners was also validated. The approach is appropriate since it has been proven statistically. Some students in the Democratic Republic of Congo have two mother tongues while others have multiple ones. The researcher suggests that the Democratic Republic of Congo join other nations in transforming education systems by incorporating one or two national languages into the education system to promote native languages at the same level as foreign languages, as is the case in many English-speaking Asian and two African countries (China, Russia and South Africa).

The transformation of the education system in the Democratic Republic of Congo suddenly poses another problem for some lecturers and this study will allow us to suggest concrete solutions to review the country's language policy and we hope that future students will benefit from it, especially from a linguistic perspective in learning of a foreign language in the classrooms.

We understand that despite the discussions surrounding our local languages, it is clear that our languages play a vital, even essential role, as they are typically the mother tongues of our students. The findings from the survey and interviews support this, as illustrated in the table below.

The campus setting is indeed multilingual, making it rare to find a student who speaks only one language. They switch between languages based on the situation and the individuals they interact with (family members in one language, colleagues in another, at church or the market in a different language, etc.).

It is logical that if we were to consider transitioning to a multilingual approach, it could significantly improve the academic performance of our students, both at the university and higher education levels. This would be a new initiative implemented universally, not just at University of Kinshasa but also at other universities in the Democratic Republic of Congo. Some may view this as a weakness, believing that students will be less proficient when expressing themselves in a foreign language.

However, the reality is quite different, as it actually enhances their abilities, as stated by some scientists and supported by the literature review. Therefore, let us embark on this new experience and observe the outcomes the surveyed and interviewed respondents expressed in their views as shown in the following table presented early:

Views of the participants triangulated

Views	Survey questionnaire		Interview	
	Frequency	Percent	Frequency	Percent
French andLingala while learning English is helpful,	15	15.0		
French is necessary while learning English	4	4.0		
French and Lingala serve as a bridge for understanding English, a foreign language			3	20.0
Other languages are importantwhile teaching or learning English, There are words which better expressed in our national languages,			2	13.3

It is clear that Mother tongues have a significant impact on English language learning and teaching in the Democratic Republic of Congo especially at the University of Kinshasa. When we observe how Congolese EFL students use their mother tongues when learning English as a foreign language.

Furthermore, this research suggests the use of the translanguaging method to assist struggling students in comprehending lessons more effectively, while also enabling instructors to effortlessly convey scientific knowledge from teaching materials that are consistently written in a foreign language, specifically English. The present world is undergoing numerous transformations, particularly in the field of education, as evident in certain countries. However, it is important to acknowledge that not all Congolese scientists may embrace this method due to personal reasons, although it presents numerous advantages that should be considered.

The new system (LMD) recommended by the Ministry in charge of Education has the potential to be implemented in the education system of the Democratic Republic of Congo, despite conflicting opinions among some lecturers. Research data undeniably shows that mother tongues play a significant role in the learning and teaching process. In the Democratic Republic of Congo, most students primarily use local languages, each employed in different circumstances.

The foreign language instructor should utilize the students' mother tongue in specific situations, such as comparing English grammar with the grammar of their mother tongue.

Allowing the use of the mother tongue in the classroom can help beginners make faster progress. Furthermore, translation exercises can be beneficial when students face difficulties with specific grammar concepts. As highlighted by McKay (2002), there is no universally applicable method that suits every context.

It is strongly advised to use translanguaging to strengthen comprehension at the level of instruction in classrooms and make sure students are getting what it is being taught. Teachers should see translanguaging as a valid pedagogical method. Translanguaging is a method that allows students to use their mother tongues while learning the target language.

It is an effective way to support English teaching by incorporating the use of local languages. In the classroom, teachers should make sure not to discriminate against students who do not speak Lingala as their language of instruction, as it has a significant influence in the region. Instead, they should recognise the importance of local languages as a means of communication that can greatly improve literacy in Lingala.

Research has shown that adopting a multilingual approach greatly improves students' access to education, fosters literacy development, and facilitates language learning. However, using the mother tongue as the medium of instruction is not widely practiced. There are several challenges that arise when using mother tongues as languages of instruction, including the following:

1. In some cases, there may not be a written form available for the native language.
2. The language may not always be recognized as a legitimate language by the majority of people.
3. It may still be necessary to develop specific terminology for teaching in the native language.
4. Finding educational resources in the native language can be challenging.
5. Providing education in multiple native languages can pose difficulties.
6. There may be a shortage of adequately trained teachers for mother tongue instruction.
7. Teaching in the mother tongue may encounter resistance from parents, teachers, and students.

In conclusion, adopting a multilingual approach enables English as a Foreign Language (EFL) teachers to collaborate with sociolinguists.

These experts interact with learners in their social lives and identify their ideal mother tongues. The findings from this collaboration will greatly support EFL teachers in their teaching practices experience.

RECOMMENDATIONS

Recommendations to the Ministry of Education

The first recommendation is directed at the Government of the Democratic Republic of Congo, inspired by insights from Professor Raoul Ekwampok. He highlights the need to nurture a passion for our languages and culture by promoting the use of African languages. This involves elevating our national languages to official status and integrating them into various sectors such as education, legal systems, media, government, and business. We should teach these languages as essential learning tools rather than mere subjects. Educated Congolese individuals should be proficient in at least two of our national languages. Schools should mandate bilingual education, with foreign languages taught alongside our own, similar to practices during colonization.

This strategy must be effective, consistent, and adapted to our country's unique size and requirements. Furthermore, a new law should be established to ensure resources are allocated for teaching our four national languages. We also need to make tools for promoting, marketing, and preserving Congolese culture readily available. Lastly, we should re-establish the Language Observatory to develop a language policy that aligns with the realities of Congolese life and shields us from Western imperialism and other colonial influences. The diversity of languages in our education system can pose challenges, particularly in creating curricula and teaching materials. Students should learn in a language they comprehend or speak. At the university level, students tend to excel when instructed in their native language.

Recommendations to EFL teachers

Investing in language education at the university level is very important. Students should learn in both their native language and a foreign language, while their academic progress should be tracked to see if they are improving. Teaching children English along with local languages helps most students understand the lessons better.

Making the national language the main language of the university also improves access to culture. It is essential for everyone to have equal educational opportunities, respecting their language and cultural background. However, this doesn't mean that students need to learn the same ideas and languages as those in other countries. Learning should happen in the language that the child knows best.

Recommendations to further researchers

It is important for local communities to receive materials in their own language, considering their unique situations. We need to change the way we educate to include everyone, no matter their background, whether they live in cities or rural areas, or come from rich or poor families. Freire (1970) mentioned that personalized learning helps people gain power and free their minds from colonial education. By sharing resources and making language accessible, we can improve everyone's quality of life. If these suggestions are put into action, they could help the university tackle some issues related to UNESCO's recommendation that children learn best in their native language. I strongly encourage the University of Kinshasa to take the initiative, especially in the English courses.

BIBLIOGRAPHY

Adebayo, D.O. (2008). The impact of mother tongue on students' achievement in English Junior secondary Certificate Examination in Western Nigeria. University of Ibadan: Ibadan.

Adekunie, M. (2022). The classical test or item response measurement theory: The status of the framework at the examination council of Lesotho. International journal of Learning, Teaching and Educational Research. 21, 8, 384-406.

Aydogan, H. & Akbarov, A. (2014). The four basic language skills, whole language & integrated skill approach in mainstream University classrooms in Turkey. Mediterranean Journal of social sciences: Edo.

Ahuja, R. (2009). Research methods. Rawat publications: Jaipur.

Alby, S. & Leglise, I. (2018). 'Multilingualism and translanguaging as a resource for teaching and learning in French Guiana in Education. Palgrave MacMillan: London.

Alejaldre, L. (2013). Status of Indigenous languages within Gambian Education Policy: English vs Vernacular languages as the vehicular language in formal education context. 5th European conference on African studies. (ECAS, 27-29 June) University of Gambia: Banjul.

Al-Hinai, M. (2011). The use of the L1 in the elementary English language classroom. Classroom Research in English Language Teaching in Oman. Sultanate of Oman: Ministry of Education, 8-14: Oman.

Amidon, Edmund, J. (1967). The role of the teacher in the classroom: A manual for understanding and improving teachers' classroom behavior.

Association for Productive Teaching: New York.

Anderson, A. (2018). English mother tongue instruction. Hidden curriculum and heteroglossic repertoires. Published PhD Thesis. Lund University: Stockholm.

Angell,B & Townsend,L. (2021). Designing and conducting mixed methods studies.

Aging research of Rutgers: New Jersey.

Workshop for 2011 society for social work and research annual meeting.

Atkinson, D. (1987). The mother tongue in the classroom: A neglected resource?

ELT Journal: Glasgow.

Atkinson, D. (1993). Teaching in the target language: a problem in the current

Orthodoxy. The Language Learning journal 8(1), 2-5.

ELT Journal: London.

Auerbach, E. R. (1993). Re-examining English only in the ESL classroom.

TESOL Quarterly 27.1, 9–32. Accessed January 31,2023.

Aydogan, H. & Akbarov,A. A. (2014). The Four Basic Language skills , whole language & integrated skill Approach in mainstream University Classrooms in Turkey.

5, 9,Mediterranean Journal of Social Sciences: Roma.

Babajide,A. & Oluranti,A.(2013) Contributions of Mother Tongue education in early childhood education

1st Annual International Interdisciplinary Conference: Azores.

Bajqinca, N. (2017). Mother Tongue Education: The Interest of a Nation. Published PhD Thesis. University of Gothenburg; Stockholm.

Balakova, L. (2013). The Use of Mother Tongue in EFL classes. Masaryk University BRNO. Published PhD Thesis: Prague.

Banerjee, S. (2021). An Introduction to classical test theory, Assessment resources. Azim Premji University: Bengaluru.

Basir, U.P.M. (2019). Multilingual approach in the nonverbal interaction model (Sociolinguistic study). Surabaya State University: Surabaya.

9, 8. International journal of Humanities and Social sciences.

Doi: 10.30845. ISSN 2220-8488(Print) available at https: www.ijhssnet.com.

Beka, M. (2016). Mother Tongue as Medium of Instruction: Benefits and challenges, International journal of Innovative languages, Literature and Art studies.4, 16-26. Seahi publications: Halaba.

Bekrieva, D. (2004). The Impact of multilingualism & language learning experiences on an immigrant woman's identity: A case study. Published Master's thesis. Iowa State University: Iowa.

Benson, C. (2010). How multilingual African contexts are pushing educational research and practice in new directions. Language and Education. 24(4), 323-336. Doi: 10.1080/09500781003678704.

Biswabandan, B. (2012). The silent class: Does multilingual education make a difference? Saarbrucken: LAP.

Biswabandan, B. (2020). Multilingual Education in Classrooms with Multiple Mother Tongues: A Case study of Pedagogical Possibilities. PhD Thesis, University of Toronto: Toronto.

Blaxter, L. et al. (2006). How to research. Open University (Maiden head & New York). British Journal of educational technology: Buckingham.

Bokamba, E. (1991). French colonial language policies in Africa and their legacies.D. Marshall(Ed) language Planning: Focus Schrift in Honor of Joshua A. Fishman. John Benjamins: Amsterdam.

Boru, T. (2018). Research Design and Methodology. Published PhD Thesis. University of South Africa: Pretoria.

Bower, G.H & Hilgard, E.R. (1981). Theories of learning. Englewood Cliffs N.J.Prentice-Hill Chicago.University of Chicago: Chicago.

Brakpan, M. (2021).Translanguaging as a pedagogical strategy to implement multilingual language policy at a South African University. Published Master's thesis at the University of Free State: Bloemfontein.

Brooks-Lewis, K. A. (2009). Adult learners' perceptions of the incorporation of their L1 in foreign language teaching and learning. Applied Linguistics 30.2, 216–235: Canterbury.

Buhendwa, F. (2010). 'Multilingualism in DRC. English Rising in a predominant Francophone Environment'. In Review of Applied languages and communication. 6, 83-109: London.

Buhendwa, F. (2010). 'Multilingualism, Family and educational issues in the

Congolese context in Revue des Langues vivantes et Communication. 6, (2),85-109: Kinshasa.

Buhendwa, F. (2011). 'Multilingualism, family and educational issues in the Congolese context. In Annales de la Faculté des Lettres et Sciences humaines , IX, 75-94 : Kinshasa.

Buhmann, D. & Trudell, B. (2008). Mother Tongue Matters: Local language as a key to effective learning.UNESCO: Paris.

Bunrosy, L. (2023). Evolution of English language teaching (ELT) methodologies and contemporary trends: A critical analysis of the Combodia context.European journal of English Language Teaching, 9(6):Bucharest.

Burdujan, R. (2020). Role of mother tongue use in foreign language classroom. 4th International conference on Modern Research in Education, Teaching and Learning. Tiraspol State University: Chisinau.

Butzkamm, W. (2003). We only learn language once. The role of the mother tongue in FL classrooms: Death of a dogma. Aachen University. Language Learning Journal 28,(1), 29–39 :Aachen.

Calvet, L. (1987) La guerre des langues et les politiques linguistiques. Payot: Paris.

Cappelleri, J.C. (2014). Overview of Classical test theory and item response theory for the quantitative assessment of items in developing patient. Reported outcomes measures. Elsevier Journals: Connecticut.

Carless, D. (2008). Student use of the mother tongue in the task-based classroom. Shiraz University. ELT Journal 62(4), 331–338: Shiraz.

Chebet, E. (2020). Influence of mother tongue usage on acquisition of literacy skills in rural early childhood development education centres in Nandi County (Nairobi). Published Thesis, Kisii University: Kisii.

Chimhundu, H. (1997). Languages policies in Africa. Intergovernmental Conference on language policies in Africa. Final Report (revised).University of Zimbabwe: Harare.

Christa Van der Walt & Nanda Klapwijk (2015). Language of learning and Teaching in a multilingual school environment: what do Teachers think? Language matters. Routledge Taylor & Francis group. Stellenbosch University: Stellenbosch.

Chumbow, B.S. (1984), 'Foreign Language Learning in a multilingual setting: the predictability of the Mother Tongue effect', IRAL, 22(4)287-296: Yaoundé.

Cissy, A. (2017) .The Influence of mother tongue on learners' performance in written English at primary level: A case study of Semuto Subcounty, Nakaseke District Kampala International University: Kampala.

Coady,J. & Huckin,T. (1997). Second language vocabulary acquisition. A rationale for pedagogy. Cambridge University Press: Cambridge.

Cochran, W.G. (1963). Sampling Techniques, 2nd Ed, John Wiley and Sons, In: New York.

Cohen, L. & Manion, L. (1989). Research methods in education. Routledge: London.

Cohen, L. et al (2011). Research Methods in education. Routledge: New York. ISBN 978-0-415-58336.

Cook, V. (2001). Using the first language in the classroom. Canadian Modern language Review, 57(3), 404-423: Toronto.

Cook, V. (2010). Translanguaging in language teaching: An argument for Reassessment. Oxford University Press: Oxford.

Creese, A. & Blackledge, A. (2010). Translanguaging in the bilingual classroom: A pedagogy for learning and Teaching? The Modern language Journal, 94, (1). 103-115: Leicester.

Creswell, J.W. (2007). Qualitative inquiry & Research Design: Choosing among five approaches. University of Nebraska. Sage publications. California: Lincoln.

Creswell, J.W. (2009). Research Design. Qualitative and Quantitative and Mixed Methods approaches. Sage publications, University of Nebraska-Lincoln: Lincoln.

Creswell, J.W. & Plano Clark (2011). Designing and Conducting Mixed Methods Research. 2nd Edition, Sage Publication: Los Angeles.

Creswell, J. W. (2014). Research design: qualitative, quantitative, and mixed methods approaches. Sage publications: Los Angeles

Creswell, J.W. & Plano Clark (2018). Designing and Conducting

Mixed Methods Research. 3nd Edition, Thousand Oaks,

C A: SagePublications: Los Angeles.

Croizier, C. (1991). Politique linguistique et developpement. Approches francophone et Anglophone: Le cas du Benin et du Nigeria. Master's thesis in sociolinguistics. Université des Sciences Humaines:

Strasbourg.

Cummins, J. (2007). Rethinking monolingual instructional strategy in multilingual classroom. Canadian journal of applied linguistics: Toronto.

Dahal, S. (2020). Teacher experiences on using Mother tongue in second language classroom: A narrative inquiry. Published PhD. Thesis. Tribhuvan University: Kathmandu.

Dawit, D.A (2020). An overview of data analysis and interpretation in research. International journal of Academic research in Education and review. 8(1), 1-27.

Deller, S. & Rinvolucri, M. (2002). Using the mother tongue: Making the most of the learner's language. English Teaching Professional & Addlestone: Delta Publishing: London.

Deller, S. (2003). Using the mother tongue. Humanizing language teaching. Sage publications. Available at https:www.deltapublishing.co.uk.

De Glabert, P. (2019). Learning in Multilingual Contexts: Language Policies, cross-linguistic transfer, and Reading Interventions. Harvard Graduate school of Education: Boston.

Delanaye,P. (1955). De l'emploi des langues dans l'enseignement des 'Africains du Congo Belge. Dans le Zaire, 9(3):227-259.

Denzin, N.K & Lincoln, Y.S. (2000). Introduction: The discipline and practice of qualitative research. In N.K. Denzin, N. & Lincoln, Y.S.(Eds). Handbook of qualitative research (2nd ed, 1-34). Thousand Oaks, CA: Sage publications.

Dicamilla, F. (1999). Socio-cognitive functions of L1 collaborative interaction in the second language classroom. The Modern Language Journal.

Dikila, S. (2016). The Use of Mother tongue in Teaching English at primary level. Published Ph D Thesis. Tribhuvan University: Kathmandu.

Djamarah, S.B. (2001). Psikologi Belajar. Rineka Cipta: Jakarta.

Djamarah, S.B & Zain, A. (2010). Strategi Belajar Mengajar (4th ed). Rineka Cipta: Jakarta.

Dodson, C. J. (1972). Language teaching and the bilingual method (2nd ed.).

Pitman: London.

Duff, P. (2008). Case study research in applied Linguistics.

Taylor & Francis: New York.

Dornyei, Z. (2010). Research methods in applied linguistics.

Oxford University Press: Oxford.

Duma, L. (2021). An analysis of multilingualism as an approach to language – in-Education policies of the Department of Bask Education in Relation to the promotion of indigenous languages as language of teaching and learning. University of Kwa-Zulu Natal: Durban.

Durkheim, E. (2004). Translation of 1884a by Neil Gross and Robert Alun Jones. Durkheimian studies. UK: Cambridge University Press: Cambridge.

Ebe, A.E. (2003). Indigenous Language: A Better Medium of Instruction for Primary Education in a Democratic Nigeria. A Paper presented at the

2nd Annual National conference of Faculty of Education.

Eberhard, D.M et al. (2020). Ethnologue: Languages of the World (23rd ed.) SIL International. http:/www.ethnologue.com /guides.

Edwards,V. (2009). Learning to be literate. Mulltilingual perspectives. Multilingual matters : Clevedon.

Ekwampok, R. (2023). Intégration des langues nationales dans le système éducatif de la RDC : problèmes et solutions possibles. Article Publié au Centre de recherche en éducation, Université Saint Augustin : Kinshasa.

Ellis, R. (1997). Second language acquisition.Oxford University Press : Oxford.

Enama, P. R.B. (2016). The impact of English-only and bilingual approaches to EFL instruction on low –achieving bilinguals in Cameroon : An empirical study. Journal of Language Teaching and Research. 7,(1),19-30 : Yaoundé.

Enquakone, E. (2019). Effects of using planned mother tongue on EFL students'speaking performance: The case of Adisskidame general and preparatory school, grade 11th focus. Bahir Dar University: Amhara.

Faizin, A. (2015). Sociolinguistics in language teaching. Journal of language teaching and Learning Mabasan, 9(2), 66-77: Batu.

Fafunwa, A.B. (1975). Education in the mother tongue. A Nigerian Experiment. The six year (Yoruba Medium) Primary Education Project at the University of Ile-Ife, Nigeria. West African journal of Education. 19(2)13-217: Osun.

Fathi, S. (2023). "Official or National language''. In Jadir, M.(ed) Recherches en Litterature,Traductologie et Linguistique .Editions Universitaires Européennes. Hassan II University: Casablanca.

Ferguson, G. (2003). 'Classroom code switching in postcolonial contexts: Functions, attitudes and policies. AILA Review 16(1), 38-51.

Fishman, J. (1972). The sociology of language. Rowley, Newbury House publishers: Philadelphia.

Forman, R. (2012). Six functions of bilingual EFL teacher talk: animating, translating, explaining, creating, prompting and dialoguing. RELC Journal, 43(2), 239-253: Singapore.

Forman, R. (2015). L1 use in EFL classes with English-only policy: Insights from triangulated data. Center for educational policy studies. English language studies Journal. 5, (2) 159-175: Urmia.

Available at www.researchgate.net.

Forteza, F. & Korneeva, L. (2017). The Mother tongue in the foreign language: An account of Russian L2 Learner's error incidence on output. The European journal of Social and Behavioural sciences: Ekaterinburg.

Freire, P. (2006). Pedagogy of the oppressed: 30th anniversary edition. The Continuum International Publishing Group Inc: New York.

French, M. (2018). Multilingual and translanguaging pedagogies in EALD. Melbourne: Languages and Multicultural Education Resource Centre. (LMERC): Melbourne.

Gabrielatos, C. (2001). L1 use in ELT: Not a skeleton but a bone of contention. A response to Prodromon. TESOL Greece newsletter, 70, 6-9: Athens.

Galante, A (2019). It is time to change the way we teach English. The Conversation. Available online at: https://theconversation.com/its-time-to-change-the-way-we-teach-english-109273.

Gass, S.M & Selinker, L. (2008). Second Language Acquisition: An introduction course (3rd ed) Routledge: New York.

Garcia, O. (2009). Education, multilingualism and translanguaging in the 21st century. In T. Skutnabb-Kangas, R. Phillipson,

A . K. Mohanty & M. Panda (eds), Social justice
B. through multilingual education: Multilingual Matters: Clevedon.

Garcia, O. & Li, W. (2014). Translanguaging: Language, Bilingualism and education.

Palgrave Macmillan: London.

Garcia, O. & Flores, N. (2020). Multilingual pedagogies in practice. Routledge Taylor &

Francis group: New York.

Gass, S. M., & Selinker, L. (2008). Second language acquisition: An introductory course (3rd ed.). Routledge: New York.

Gattegno, C. (1972). Teaching foreign languages in schools: The silent way. 2nd ed. Educational solutions: New York.

Ghorbani, A. (2012). Mother tongue in the EFL classroom.

Advances in language and literary studies Journal.

Australian International Academic Centre, 3, (2), 63-75: Melbourne.

Gogolin, I, et al. (2011). Förderung von Kindern und Jugendlichen mit Migrationshintergrund FörMig. Bilanz und Perspektiven eines Modellprogramms. FörMig Edition, Bd. 7. Münster: Waxmann

Gorter, D. & Cenoz, J. (2011). A multilingual approach: Conclusions and future Perspectives: Afterword. The Modern Language Journal. (11) 442-445: Madrid.

Greggio,S. & Gil, G. (2007). Teacher's and learner's use of code –switching in the English as a foreign language classroom: a qualitative study. Linguagem and Ensino, 10(2), 371-393.

Grosjean,F. (2012). Bilingualism: A short introduction. In F. Grosjean & Pli(Eds), The psycholinguistics of bilingualism, 5-25. Hoboken, John Wiley & Sons: New Jersey.

Grosjean, F. (1985). The bilingual as a competent but specific speaker-hearer. Journal of multilingual and multicultural development. 6,467-477: New Jersey.

Gumperz, J.J. (2008). Studying language, culture, and society: Sociolinguistics or linguistic anthropology. Journal of Sociolinguistics. 12(4), 532-545: New York.

Guzula, X. et al (2016). Languaging-for-learning: Legitimising translanguaging and enabling multimodal practices in third spaces: Southern African linguistics and applied language studies. 34(3). http://www.doi.org

Han, J. & Park, K. (2017). Monolingual or bilingual approach: The effectiveness of teaching and methods in second language classroom. Purdue University: languages and cultures conference: Indiana.

Hambleton, R. K & Jones, R. W. (1993). Comparison of classical test theory and item response theory and their applications to test development. Educational measurement. Issues and practice, 12(3), 535-556:New York.

Harbord, J. (1992). The Use of the mother tongue in the classroom. ELT Journal.'46,350-355: New Jersey.

Hastjarjo, K. (2015). Strategic real estate development: Mixed Method using sequential explanatory strategy-Research Methodology. Journal of

Entrepreneurship, business and Economics. Padjadjaran University: Bandung.

Hawkins, E. W. (1987). Modern languages in the curriculum. Cambridge University Press: Cambridge.

Hawks, P. (2001). Making distinctions: A discussion of the mother tongue in the foreign language classroom. Hwa Kang Journal of TEFL, 7, 47-55.

Herkovits, M. (1948). Acculturation: The study of culture contact. Wesley college library. New York.

Hernandez, B. (2018). The Dilemmas of mother tongue education. The integration of curriculum theory and practice: Chinese Mandarin and Spanish mother tongue teachers' experiences in Sweden. Stockholm Universitet: Stockholm.

Heug, K et al (2017). Multilingualism and translanguaging in the teaching of and through English: Rethinking linguistic boundaries in an Australian

University. Dordrecht, Springer: Cham.

Heug, K.et al. (2019). Using multilingual approach moving from theory to practice. A resource book of strategies, activities and projects for the classroom. British Council: London.

Hinmassia, R. (2014). Language choice and attitudes in public institutions: The Case of the University of Maroua. European Journal of English language and literature, 12,(6), 1-18. : Maroua. Print ISSN: 2055 - 0138.

Holmes, J. (2001). Introduction to sociolinguistics (2nd ed) Longman:London

Holmes,J. (2013). An Introduction to Sociolinguistics (4th ed) Routledge: Oxon.

Hornby, A.S. (1995). Oxford Advanced Learner's Dictionary of Current English, Oxford University Press: Oxford.

Hudson, R.A. (1988). Sociolinguistics. Cambridge University Press: New York.

Hymes, D. H. (1974). Foundations of sociolinguistics: An ethnographic approach. University of Pennsylvania Press: Philadelphia.

Ivankova, N. & Creswell, J. (2006). Using mixed-methods sequential explanatory design: From theory to Practice. Sage publications. University of Nebraska: Lincoln.

Jones, B.D. (2010). An examination of motivation model components in face-to-face and online instruction. Retrieved from https: www.psycnet.apa.org.

Jones, B.D. (2010). Strategies to implement a motivation model and increase student engagement. Paper presented at the annual meeting of the APA psycnet. Retrieved from https:www.psycnet.apa.org.

Kamwangamalu, Nkonko.M. (1996). The Colonial legacy and language planning in Sub Sahara Africa: The Case of Zaire, applied linguistics. 18, 69-85, Cambridge University Press: Cambridge.

Kamwangamalu, Nkonko.M. (2010).Vernacularization, globalization and language economics in non-English-speaking countries in Africa. Language Problems and language Planning. John Benjamins publishing company: Amsterdam.

Kamwangamalu, Nkonko.M. (2010). Multilingualism and Codeswitching in education. In: Nancy H Hornberger and Sandra Lee McKay and Nancy Hornberger (eds) Sociolinguistics and language Education. Multilingual Matters: Bristol.

Kamwangamalu, Nkonko.M. (2011). Language planning: Approaches and methods.In: Eli Hinkel (ed.) The Handbook of Research in Second language planning and learning, Volume II. Routledge: New York.

Kapalu, K. (2015). Familiar language Versus Mother Tongue: An Analysis of the implications of the current language of instruction policy in Zambia. International journal of Zambia Zango 31, 65-77. University of Zambia: Lusaka.

Kaplan, R. & Baldauf, R. (1997). Language planning: From practice to theory. Multilingual matters: Clevedon.

Kerr, P. (2019). The use of L1 in English language teaching. Part of the Cambridge papers in ELT series. Cambridge University Press: Cambridge.

Khanday, S.A. (2019). The research design. Journal of critical reviews. 6(3),2:

Kuala lumpur.

Khati, A.R. (2011). When and why of mother tongue use in English classroom. Nepali English language teachers' association: Journal of NELTA, Nepal journals online: 16, 1-2. : Kathmandu.

Kidinda, C. (2021). Influence of learners' mother tongue on the learning of English as a foreign language. Bachelor's thesis. University of Kinshasa: Kinshasa.

Kilumba, K et al. (2013). Le Katanga linguistique. Projet de recherché sur 3 langues autochtones face au development: Katanga.

Kim, S.Y. (2002). Teachers' perceptions about teaching English through English. English Teaching .1, 131–148. Hanyang University: Seoul.

Kim, S.Y. (2008). Five years of teaching English through English: Responses from teachers and prospects for learners. English Teaching .1, 51–70. Hanyang University: Seoul.

Kithaka, M. (2016). Mother Tongues as media of Instruction: The case of Kenya. The University of Nairobi journal of language and linguistics. 5, 45-59. University of Nairobi: Nairobi.

Kitzinger, A.I. (2015). Multilingual and multicultural challenges in a Hungarian Kindergarten. Published PhD Thesis. Pazmany Peter catholic University: Budapest.

Kombo, D. K (2005). Research methods. Ad print publishers, Kenyatta University: Nairobi.

Kothari, C.R. (2004). Research methodology: Methods and techniques. 2nd Edition, New Age International Publishers: New Delhi.

Kobia, J. (2017). Mother tongue Education in Kenya: Significance, challenges and prospects in a multilingual situation. Journal of contemporary Research, 14, 141-165. University of Swaziland: Kwaluseni.

Koucka, A. (2007). The Role of Mother Tongue in English language teaching.

Published PhD Thesis, University of Pardubice: Prague

Krashen, S. D. (1981). Second language acquisition and second language learning.

Pergamon: Oxford.

Krashen, S. D. (1985). The input hypothesis: Issues and implications.

Longman: London.

Krishnaji, N. (1990). The mother tongue in the classroom: A neglected resource?

ELT Journal, 44(4), 274-281: Indah Maslahah.

Kruger, J.A. (2010). Accommodating and promoting multilingualism through blended learning. Published PhD thesis. North-west University: Johannesburg.

Kumar, K. (2011). Research Methodology. A step-by-step guide for beginners. Sage publications Ltd: New Delhi.

Kuper, W. (2003).The necessity of introducing mother tongues in education systems of developing countries. In Ouane(Ed) Towards a Multilingual culture of Education, 89-102. UNESCO Institute of Education: Hamburg.

Langa, M. & Sesati, M. (2006). Students' views on the use of home language for teaching. Paper presented at the 14th Annual SAARMSTE conference. University of Pretoria: Pretoria.

Lapdate,R, & Kshirsagar,J. (2021). Single random sampling. In book: Advanced sampling methods. 11-35.

Larsen-Freeman, D. (2000). Techniques and principles in language teaching (2nd ed.). Oxford University Press: Oxford.

Lee, J.-H. (2007). Where to start teaching English through English: Based on perceived effectiveness of teachers' English use. English Teaching 62.4, 335–354: Seoul.

Leedy, P.D. (1997). Practical research: Planinig and design. (6th edition). Prentice-hall: New jersey.

Li, M. (2020). Vernacular: Its features, relativity, functions and social significances. International Journal of Literature and Arts, Special issue: 8, (2), 81-86, School of Interpreting and Translation studies, Guangzhou University of foreign studies: Guangzhou.

Lightbown,P. (2004). Commentary. What to teach? How to teach? In B. Van Pattu(ed.). Processing instruction: Mahwah, 65-78: New Jersey.

Lightbown,P. & Spada, N.M.(2013). How languages are learned. (3rd ed).Oxford University Press: Oxford.

Lindholm-Leary, K.J. (2001). Dual language education. Multilingual Matters: Clevedon.

Linh, H. T & Hoi, H.T (2020). The need to use mother tongue in communication of ethnic students. Journal of critical reviews. 7,(15),5970-5974. Thai

Nguyen University of Education: Hanoi.

Littlewood, W. T. (1981). Communicative language teaching. Cambridge University Press: Cambridge.

Littlewood, W. (1999). Second language teaching methods. In Spolsky, B. (ed.), concise encyclopedia of educational linguistics. Elsevier, 658–668: Amsterdam.

Littlewood,W. & Shufang, W.(2022). The Role of Learners' first language in the Foreign Language Classroom. Language Teaching Research Quaterly Journal. Vol 31, pp 174-182. Hong Kong Baptist University : Hon Kong.

Little,D. & Kirwana,D. (2018). Translanguaging as a key to educational success : The experience of one Irish primary school.In P. Van Avermaet, S. Slambrouck, K.Van Grop, S. Sierens and K. Maryns(Eds). The multilingual edge of education, 313-240, Pelgrave Macmillan : London.

Lubudi, B. (2023). Promotion des langues nationales et développement culturel : pour un patriotisme linguistique non obscurantiste. Centre de Recherche Pédagogique, Université Saint Augustin : Kinshasa.

Luzitusu, M.T. (2020). Investigating on the mother tongue : Case of Kindele district.Unpublished bacherlor's thesis. University of Kinshasa : Kinshasa.

Mahmud, S. (2018). Should teachers use L1 in EFL classroom? Journal of NELTA. 23, (1-2), 25-39: Kathmandu.

Mahmutoglu, H. and Kicir, Z. (2013). The Use of Mother Tongue in EFL classrooms. Journal of Social sciences. University of Lefke: Gujarat.

Makoni, R. (2016). The Relationship between Mother Tongue and English second language learning strategies. Published Master's thesis. University of Witwatersrand: South Africa.

Malekani, C.W. (2023). La langue d'élite comme langue maternelle dans un environnement multilingue : Le cas du français au plateau des résidents, Unikin, RDC. Centre de Recherche Pédaogique, Université Saint Augustin: RDC.

Malekani, C.W. (2023). Mother Tongues and Teaching English as a Foreign Language: A case study. Published paper in Russian scientific journal of pedagogical linguistics: Russia.

Malekani, K. (1987). 'English as a Fourth Language: its phonological Acquisition by Zairean students multilingual in Kiswahili, Lingala and French, PhD Dissertation, University of Exeter.

Malekani, K. (2001). 'English and the Mother Tongue effect in the Democratic Republic of Congo, Revue RASE, (2), 61-71.

Malekani, K. (2002). Utilisation des langues en RDC: Cas des étudiants à Kisangani et de Kinshasa. L'Observatoire des langues.(1),51-63: Kinshasa.

Malekani, K. & Nsimambote, Z. (2012). Identifying Mother Tongues in a Multilingual setting in Mouvement et Enjeux sociaux. 4, 81- 88.

Malekani, K. (2012). Le legs Colonial et la planification linguistique au Zaïre /Congo la Revue des langues Vivantes et communication. 7, 81- 88 :Kinshasa.

Mallikarjun, B.(2002). A Multilingual Approach Towards Language Teaching in Indian schools. 2, 1-4.   . Central Institute of Indian Languages : Mysuru.

Mankana, B. (2023) Repenser le système éducatif Congolais sur le modèle de l'Egypte ancienne. Article publié au Centre de Recherche Pédagogique, 1(2),11-226.Université Saint Augustin : Kinshasa.

Mansor, R. (2017). The Use of the Mother Tongue in the teaching of English as a foreign language in Libyan Higher Education. Published Thesis. Manchester Metropolitan University: Manchester.

Mansory, M. (2019). Exploring teachers 'beliefs and practices on the use of the mother tongue as a mediational tool in a Saudi EFL classroom. Arab world English Journal. Special issue I: Application of global ELT practices in Saudi Arabia, 72-86.

Marshall, H. (2002). What do we do when we code data? Qualitative Research Journal. 56-70: Melbourne.

Matthews, P.H. (2007). The concise oxford dictionary of Linguistics: Oxford University Press: Oxford.

McCombes, S. (2019). Understanding Different Sampling Methods.

https://www.scribbr.com/methodology/sampling-methods.

Mc Glym, C. (2013). Language in Education Policy and Practice in Post-colonial Africa: An Ethnographic case study of the Gambia. PhD Thesis: Banjul.

Mc Milan, B.A. (2011). The practice of policy: teacher attitudes toward 'English only'. 39(2), 251-263. Available at https:www.researchgate.net.

Mc Millan, J. H.& Schumacher, S. (2006). Research in education: Evidence – based inquiry (6th ed). Allyn and Bacon: Boston. Available at https:www.scirp.org.

Mebratu, B. (2016). Mother Tongue as a Medium of Instruction: Benefits and Challenges, International Journal of Innovative language, literature & Art studies: Seahi publications. Wolaita Soto University: Addis Abeba.

Mello, h. a. b. (2004): Madrinha ou Madrasta? O Papel da L1 na

Aquisição de L2. Signótica - Revista do Programa de Pós-Graduação em

Letras e Linguística da Universidade Federal de Goiás. 16,(2), 213-242: Goiânia, Disponível em: http://www.revistas.ufg.br.

Meyer,M. et al (2016). Making use of multiple (non-shared) first languages: state of and need for research and development in the European language context. Retrieved from http.www.researchgate.net.

Mitits, L. (2016). Language learning strategy profile of monolingual and multilingual EFL learners. Paper presented at the International symposium on Theoretical and Applied linguistics. University of Thrace. 698-713(ISTAL 21): Thrace. ISSN 2529-1114.

Moeller, A.K. & Catalano, T. (2015) Foreign language Teaching and Learning. International Encyclopedia of the Social & Behavioral sciences, second edition, Faculty Publications, University of Nebraska-Lincoln: Lincoln.

Mohanty,A.K. (2008). Multilingual education in India. In J. Cumming & N.H. Hornberger (Eds). Vol5, Bilingual education. Encyclopedia of language and education. (2nd ed) pp 165-174. Springer: New York.

Molokommel, N.B. (2020). The Effects of Multilingualism on Mother Tongue

Acquisition. Published Master's thesis. University of South Africa: Pretoria.

Moyo, T. (2001). The changing language policies and reversing language roles in Malawi: from colonial Times (1891-1964) to the present. University of Zululand: Kwazulu-Natal.

Mubangu, I. (2023). English language teaching and curriculum development. Published book. Livres pour les grands lacs: Kinshasa.

Mubiayi Mamba, A. (2013). Apport du psychologue clinicien en milieu hospitalier, XII, 3, psychologie et société nouvelle. Centre de Recherche et d'Action sociale. Université de Kinshasa : Kinshasa.

Muhammad, R. (2017). Impact of Mother tongue on learning English language on secondary school level students. Journal of literature, languages and linguistics: New Delhi.

Mujere, N. (2016). Sampling in research: Mixed methods research for improved scientific study. IGI global scientific publishing: Pennsylvania.

Mularsih, P.S & Satyarini, E. (2022). Using Mother Tongue in EFL classrooms: Pros and Cons. Journal of Applied Linguistics Indonesia (Aplinesia), 6(1), 26-32: Surabaya.

Mumbembe, L. et al. (2015). Language challenges facing students from the Democratic Republic of Congo in a University in South Africa. International journal of Education and Science, 8(3) 597-604: Pretoria.

Mutombo,Huta-Mukana(1979). Variétés des idiomes et l'enseignement en langues zairoises. Maadini: 22, 32-41: Kinshasa.

Mutombo,Huta-Mukana(1987). Pour une politique educative en langues nationales linguistique et sciences humaines 27: 37-40: Kinshasa.

Mutombo, Huta-Mukana (2012). La problematique des langues dans les systemes educatifs en Afrique. 10, (14), 131-137. Fahrenhouse. Centre de linguistique theoretique et appliquée. (CELTA): Kinshasa.

Nakayiza, J. (2013). The Sociolinguistics of multilingualism in Uganda: A case study of the official language policy, planning and management of Luruuri –Lunyara and Luganda. Published PhD Thesis, University of London: London.

Nation, P. (2001). Learning vocabulary in another language. Victoria University of Wellington. Cambridge University Press: Cambridge.

Nation, P. (2001). The role of the first language is foreign language learning. Asian EFL journal, 5(2),1-8: Singapore.

Natukunda, V. (2013). The influence of mother tongue on learner's performance in written English at primary level: A Case study of Nakawa Division. Published Bachelor's thesis. Kampala International University : Kampala.

Ndolo, Menayame, J. A. (1992). Language situation, language planning and nationhood : The case of Zaire. Linguistic TESOL. Unpublished Doctoral dissertation, State University of New York : New York.

Ngoie, I. (2015). Le français à Lubumbashi: Usages et representations. Published PhD Thesis. Nice Sophia University: Nice.

Nkulu, K. (1984). Alternative grammatical analyses of Zairean copperbelt Swahili: Some refutations and phrase structure.

University of York: York.

Nordlie, S. (2019). Approaches to multilingualism. A study of Norwegian student teachers 'knowledge experience and attitudes. Published Master's Thesis. University of Bergen: Bergen.

Norris, L. (2019). Using multilingual approaches. Teaching English: British Council: London.

Novick, M.R. (1966). The axioms and principal results of Classical test theory. Journal of Mathematical Psychology, 3(1), 1-18.https: //doi.org/10.10.16/0022

Nsimambote, Z. (2014). Explanatory Notes on Quantitative Procedure Applied to Research on Mother Tongues Identification in a multilingual setting: Matinées scientifiques. CELTA: Kinshasa.

Nsimambote, Z. (2023). A Procedure Establishing Perfect Multilingualism in a community. In Revue Internationale des Dynamiques Sociales: Mouvements et enjeux Sociaux. 129, 39-46 : Kinshasa.

Nsimambote,Z. (2024). Perfect mother tongue of English learners in Kinshasa. In Cahiers Africains des droits de l'homme et de la democratie ainsique du developpement durable. Revue Africaine Interdisciplinaire 83,(1), 427-436 :Kinshasa.

Nsimambote, Z. (2024). Establishing perfect mother tongue in a multilingual setting. Conférence à la Faculté des Lettres. Université de Kinshasa: Kinshasa.

Ntahwakuderwa, B.C.(1987). Form and function in the interlanguage of Zairean learners of English.University of Edinburgh. 412 p : Edinburgh.

Numertayasa, I.W. et al. (2020) The Effects of literacy pattern and mother tongue on the language learning ability during learning from home. Journal of advanced social sciences and humanities research, 4th

International conference on language, literature culture and education: Banjarmasin.

Nunan, D. (1991). Language teaching methodology: A textbook for teachers, , Prentice Hall: New Delhi.

Nunan, D. (1991). Research Methods in language learning. Cambridge University press: Cambridge.

Nunan, D. (2003). Practical English language Teaching. McGraw Hill:Sydney.

Obim, A.J.(2022). Influence of Mother Tongue on English language use selected Mother Tongue factors affecting English language usage: A case study of Ikom local government area. European journal of English language and literature studies: London.

Odimire, F. & Ayob, S. (2020). The Utilisation of Translanguaging for learning and teaching in multilingual primary classrooms. De Gruyter Mouton Multilingual journal, 105-129: New York.

Odoyo, B. (2014). Benefits of Multilingualism in Education. Universal Journal of Educational Research 2(3):223-229. Maseno University: Maseno.

Okofo, A. (2003).'If you've got a Mother tongue, please use it'. The language of Education situation in Ghana. International journal of Innovative Research and Studies, 2(5): Cyprus.

Okoyo, A. (2013) The Influence of Mother Tongue on Learner's performance in written Kiswahili at primary level: A case study of Migori county,

Kampala international University. Published Bachelor's thesis: Kampala.

Opoola, B.T.(ed)(2002). Linguistics and Mother Tongue Teaching and Learning in Nigeria Primary schools. Oyo City immaculate Press: Oyo.

Osuji et al. (2014). General teaching Methods. Lecture notes. School of Education. National Open University of Nigeria: Lagos.

Otheguy, R. et al (2015). Clarifying translanguaging and deconstructing named languages. A Perspective from Linguistics. Applied Linguistics review, 6(3), 281-307: New York.

Otwinowska, A, K. (2011). Do we need to teach culture and how much culture do we need? University of Warsaw. In Book Aspects of culture in Second language Acquisition and Foreign language: Warsaw. Doi: 10.1007/978-642-2020.

Oyewole, O. (2017). Influence of Mother Tongue in the Teaching and Learning of English language in Selected schools in Ondo State. Nigeria Journal of Education and Practice, 8, 30: Lagos.

Ozfidan, B. (2017). Right of knowing and Using Mother Tongue: A Mixed method Study. English Language Teaching 10, (12). Canadian Center of Science and Education: Toronto.

Pacek, D. (2003). Should EFL give up on translation? Paper at the talk given at the 11th annual Korea TESOL International conference: Seoul.

Pami, M. (2023). The Use of English by students studying in English Department. Unpublished bachelor's thesis. University of Kinshasa: Kinshasa.

Pardede, P. (2018). Use of Mother Tongue in EFL classes of Secondary Schools in Jabodebeck: Students' and Teachers' Perception. Journal of English Teaching, 4, 62-80.Universitas Kristen Indonesia: Jakarta.

Phindane, P. (2015). Learning in mother tongue: Language preferences in South Africa. International journal of Education and science: Pretoria.

Phillipson, R. (1992). Linguistic imperialism. Oxford University Press: Oxford.

Polio, C. G. & Duff, P. A. (1994). Teachers' language use in university foreign language classrooms: A qualitative analysis of English and target-language alternation. The Modern Language Journal 78(3), 313–326: Vancouver.

Polit,D. & Hungler,B. (1999). Nursing research: Principle and method, 6th Lippinocott company, 416-417: Philadelphia.

Polkinghorne, D.E. (2005). Language and meaning: Data collection in qualitative research. Journal of counseling psychology. 52, (2) 137-145.

Popplewell, R. (2013). A rough guide to sampling. Intrac: Oxford.

Poulisse, N. & Bongaerts,T. (1994). First language use in second language production. Applied Linguistics. 15, (1), 36-37: Oxford.

Prace, D. (2010). Translation and the Role of the Mother Tongue in ELT.Published Diploma Thesis.Univerzita Palackeho V Olomouci: Olomouc.

Pritchard, A. (2009). Ways of learning: Learning theories and learning styles in the classroom (2nd ed) ,David Fulton Publishers: London.

Probyn, M. (2015). Pedagogical translanguaging: Bridging discourses in South

African science classrooms. Language and Education 29(3) 218-234: Cape town.

Richards, J. C. & Rodgers, T. S. (2001). Approaches and methods in language teaching (2nd ed.). Cambridge University Press: Cambridge.

Richards, J. & Schmidt, R. (2010). Longman Dictionary of Language Teaching and Applied Linguistics. (4th Ed), 644 pages. Taylor and Francis group. Routledge: London.

Samadi, M, R. (2011). Role of the L1 in FL classrooms: Learner and teacher beliefs, attitudes and practices. A Master's thesis, Kansas State University (unpublished): Topeka. Available at https: www. Krex-k-state.edu.

Saputra, B. (2021). Students' perception of Teachers 'pedagogical and personal competences toward their English learning. Published Ph.D. Thesis. State Islamic University: New Delhi.

Saville-Troike, M. (2006). Introducing Second Language Acquisition. Cambridge University Press: Cambridge.

SECCATO, M. G. (2010). A importância do uso pleno da língua inglesa durante o processo de ensino-aprendizagem nas séries iniciais do ensino fundamental. In: ROCHA; C. H.; TONELLI; J. R. A.; SILVA, K. Língua estrangeira para crianças: ensino-aprendizagem e formação docente. Campinas: Pontes Editora. 125-148

Seid, Y. (2017). The Impact of Learning in Mother Tongue First: Evidence from a Natural experiment in Ethiopia. International growth center: Addis Ababa.

Sethole, S.P. (2014). The nature and extent of Mother tongue interference by

Sepedi on the effectiveness of learning English among information Technology foundation students. Published Master's thesis. University of Pretoria: Pretoria.

Shukla, S. (2020). Research Methodology and Statistics. Rishit Publications: Ahmedabad.

Shukla, S. (2020). Concept of population and sample. In how to write a research paper? Rishit publications: Ahmedabad.

Simpson, J. (2016). Using multilingual approaches. Available online at: https://www.teachingenglish.org.uk/article/john-simpson-using-multilingual-approaches. Consulted on April 26, 2024.

Slameto (1995).Belajar dan Faktor –faktor yang Mampengaruhnya. Rineka Cipta: Jakarta.

Sinclair, J. (1987). Collins Cobuild English Language Dictionary. London.

Tsengele, J. (2012). Young learners' linguistic ability and analytical thinking in acquiring English as a second language from infancy up to 12 years old. Unpublished bachelor's thesis. University of Kinshasa: Kinshasa.

Sulaiman, M. and Hasan, S. (2017). The Influence of mother tongue on learning English language by Arab learners. International journal of scientific and research publications: New Delhi.

Tang, J. (2002). Using L1 in the English classroom. English Teaching Forum. 40(1), 36-43: Washington.

Timor, T. (2012). Use of the Mother tongue in teaching a foreign language. Journal of language Education in Asia, 3, 7-14. Kibbutzin College of Education: Tel Aviv.

Todeva, E. & Cenoz, J. (2009). The multiple realities of multilingualism. Mouton de Gruyter: Berlin.

Tom-Lawyer, O. & Thomas, M. (2024). The status of English as a medium of instruction in Sub –Saharan Africa. A systematic review of Nigeria and Tanzania. European journal of English Language Teaching. 9(1), 1-22: Bucharest.

Troike, R.C. (1978). Research evidence for the effectiveness of bilingual education. NABE journal 3(1), 13-24: New York.

Tsitsi, G.N. (2013). A Critical review of policy on language-in-Education for Africa: A Case of Zimbabwe. Published Ph.D. Thesis. University of South Africa: Pretoria.

Tukunda, H. (2023). The problem of promoting African languages. Book article published at Center for educational research, Saint Augustin University: Kinshasa.

Turabian, K.L. (2007). A manual for writers of Research papers, Theses and Dissertations. Chicago style for students and Researchers. The University of Chicago Press: Chicago.

Turnbull, M. (2001). There is a role for the L1 in second and foreign language teaching. Canadian Modern Language Review 57.4, 531–540: Toronto.

Turnbull, M. & Arnett, K. (2002). Teachers' uses of the target and first languages in second and foreign language classrooms. Annual Review of Applied Linguistics 22, 204–218: Prince Edward Island.

Twaambo, E. (2018). Research Practices of Academics in an African University setting: The case of the University of Zambia. Published PhD thesis. University of Stellenbosch: Stellenbosch.

UNESCO (1953). The Use of Vernacular Language in Education: Report of UNESCO meeting of specialists. Paris.

UNESCO (1955). The Use of Vernacular languages in Education. UNESCO: Paris.

UNESCO (2003). Education in a multilingual world. UNESCO Education position paper. Paris: UNESCO. Retrieved January 15,2023. From https: www.Unesdoc.unesdoc.org.

UNESCO (2004). Education for all: The quality imperative. EFA global Monitoring Report: Paris.

UNICEF, (1999). Mother Tongue-Based Multilingual Education in the Philippines: Studying Top-Down Policy Implementation from the Bottom Up. The state of the world's children. Author: New York.

Vagner, T.W. (2007). Introduction to research methods. Available at https://www.psychology.about.com/research methods. Accessed on july 2024.

Van Keerbergen, J. (1985). Histoire de l'enseignement catholique au Kasai. (1891-1947). Ed. De l'Archidiocese : Kananga.

Vincent, W. & Shanmugam, S.K.K. (2020). The Role of Classical Test Theory to determine the Quality of Classroom Teaching Test Items. Pedagogia: Jurnal Pendidika, 9, (1): Sidoarjo. ISSN 2548 2254(online) ISSN 2089 3833 (print).

Vireak,K & Bunrosy,L. (2024).Exploring language teaching methods: An in-depth analysis of grammar, translation, direct method, audiolingual methods: A literature review: Phnom Penh.

Wahdaniyah, J. (2017). The Effectiveness of using mother tongue toward students English comprehension. Published PhD Thesis. University of Makassar: Makassar.

Wahyuni, E.N. (2010). What is learning. In: Learning theory. Faculty of Tarbiyah and Teaching Training, Maulana Malik Ibrahim State Islamic University, Malang, 1-25. UNSPECIFIED. (Unpublished). Part of Book: Malang.

Warsame, H. (2018).Translanguaging in the English school subject. Student and teacher experiences of translanguaging as a teaching resource. University of Oslo: Ottawa.

Wetshokodi, M.O. & Cavusoglu, C. (2022). Language planning and English as a foreign language in the Democratic Republic of Congo: a scoping review. International Journal of curriculum and instruction.14 (1),1135-1147: Barcelona.

Available at :https:www. Wcci-international.org.

Wharton, C. (2007). Informed use of the mother tongue in the English

Language classroom. EUL Journal of Social Sciences. (IV:I) 49-72. Retrieved from. Http://www.birmingham.ac.uk/Journal. Accessed on November 17, 2023.

Wigglesworth, G. (2002). The role of the first language in the second language classroom: Friend or foe. English Teaching 57(1), 17–31: Seoul.

Wilkinson, A. (1991). The scientist' handbook for writing papers and dissertation. Englewood Cliffs. Prentice Hall: New Jersey.

Woolston, C& Osorio, J. (2019). When English is not your mother tongue.

Nature, 570, (7760), 265-267: Retrieved from. Http://www.researchgate.net. Accessed on August 17, 2023.

Wu, T. (2010) .Open the door to English with your native language: The Role of the mother tongue in English language teaching in China. Published PhD.Thesis. Technical University of Rhineland-Westphalia: Hamm.

Yamane, Taro (1967). Statistics: the Introductory Analysis.2nd Ed.

Harper and Row: New York.

Yates, B. A. (1980). The origins of language policy in Zaire".

The Journal of Modern African studies. 18(2), 257-279: Cambridge.

Yoasa, N. (2016). A Multilingual Education policy for South Sudan in a globalised world. Published at British Council. University of Juba: Juba.

Zamroni (2001). Paradigma Pendidikan Masa Depan. Yogyakarta: Biograf Publishing :Yogyakarta. 186 pages. Universitas Indonesia library. Available at :www.lib.ui.ac.id. ISBN :97986803411.

APPENDICES

APPENDIX A

QUESTIONNAIRE D'ENQUETE SOCIO- PSYCHOLINGUISTIQUE

Dans le cadre de la recherche doctorale, nous menons une enquête sur des langues maternelles multiples parfaites).

Veuillez nous fournir vos opinions sur l'utilisation des autres langues dans l'enseignement des cours d'anglais.

Veuillez répondre aux questions posées :

   I.   **Votre sexe**

1. Masculin
2. Féminin

II. Votre âge :

1. 18 - 25
2. 26 - 29
3. 30+

III. Quelle est la première langue apprise en famille ?

1. LINGALA
2. KIKONGO
3. CILUBA
4. KISWAHILI
5. FRANÇAIS
6. ANGLAIS
7. AUTRES (………………………)

IV. Quel est le dictionnaire préféré pour vous ?

1. LINGALA
2. 2.KIKONGO
3. 3.CILUBA
4. 4.KISWAHILI
5. 5.FRANÇAIS
6. 6.ANGLAIS
7. 7.AUTRES (………………………)

V. En quelles langues préférez-vous vous exprimer au tribunal pour mieux vous défendre ?

1. LINGALA
2. KIKONGO
3. CILUBA
4. KISWAHILI
5. FRANÇAIS
6. ANGLAIS
7. AUTRES (………………………)

VI. Lors d'une querelle, en quelles langues préférez-vous parler à la personne avec qui vous vous querellez ?

1. LINGALA
2. KIKONGO
3. CILUBA
4. KISWAHILI
5. FRANÇAIS

6. ANGLAIS

7. AUTRES (..........................)

VII. En quelles langues, lors de la communication, sentez-vous beaucoup plus à l'aise et les idées viennent d'elles-mêmes ?

1. LINGALA
2. KIKONGO
3. CILUBA
4. KISWAHILI
5. FRANÇAIS
6. ANGLAIS
7. AUTRES (..........................)

VIII. Lorsque vous êtes en difficultés et le secours est plus que nécessaire, En quelles langues criez-vous pour le secours ?

1. LINGALA
2. KIKONGO
3. CILUBA
4. KISWAHILI
5. FRANÇAIS
6. ANGLAIS
7. AUTRES (..........................)

IX. En quelles langues adressez-vous à votre partenaire pour exprimer vos intimités ?

1. LINGALA
2. KIKONGO
3. CILUBA
4. KISWAHILI

5. FRANÇAIS
6. ANGLAIS
7. AUTRES (..........................)

X. Quelles la (les) langue(s) de vos émissions télévisées ou films préférés ?

1. LINGALA
2. KIKONGO
3. CILUBA
4. KISWAHILI
5. FRANÇAIS
6. ANGLAIS
7. AUTRES (..........................)

XI. En quelles langue (s) rédigez-vous avec beaucoup plus de confiance sans avoir peur de commettre des erreurs d'orthographes ?

1. LINGALA
2. KIKONGO
3. CILUBA
4. KISWAHILI
5. FRANÇAIS
6. ANGLAIS
7. AUTRES (..........................)

XII. Quelle(s) est/sont la/les langues des ouvrages ou livres que vous lisez avec passion ?

1. LINGALA
2. KIKONGO
3. CILUBA

4. KISWAHILI
5. FRANÇAIS
6. ANGLAIS
7. AUTRES (..........................)

XIII. Lors des examens ou interrogations, en quelle(s) langue(s) réfléchissez- vous le plus souvent et qui vous aident à trouver aisément les réponses aux questions posées ?

1. LINGALA
2. KIKONGO
3. CILUBA
4. KISWAHILI
5. FRANÇAIS
6. ANGLAIS
7. AUTRES (..........................)

XIV. En quelle(s) langue(s) vos camarades vous expliquent le cours en dehors de l'auditoire ?

1. LINGALA
2. KIKONGO
3. CILUBA
4. KISWAHILI
5. FRANÇAIS
6. ANGLAIS
7. AUTRES (..........................)

XV. En quelle(s) langue(s) préférez-vous que votre pasteur vous prêche à l'église ?

1. LINGALA
2. KIKONGO
3. CILUBA
4. KISWAHILI
5. FRANÇAIS
6. ANGLAIS
7. AUTRES (...........................)

XVI. Quelle(s) langue(s) proposerez- vous qu'on puisse utiliser dans l'enseignement des cours d'anglais pour vous permettre de bien comprendre la matière ?

1. LINGALA
2. KIKONGO
3. CILUBA
4. KISWAHILI
5. FRANÇAIS
6. ANGLAIS
7. AUTRES (...........................)

XVII. Veuillez commenter sur l'utilisation des autres langues dans l'enseignement de la langue anglaise.

Merci pour votre participation !

APPENDIX B

INTERVIEW QUESTIONS

Votre sexe :

1. Masculin
2. Féminin
3. Votre âge

I. Quelle est la première langue apprise en famille ?
II. . Quel est le dictionnaire préféré pour vous ?
III. En quelles langues préférez-vous vous exprimer au tribunal pour mieux vous défendre ?
IV. Lors d'une querelle, en quelles langues préférez-vous parler à la personne avec qui vous vous querellez ?
V. En quelles langues, lors de la communication, sentez-vous beaucoup plus à l'aise et les idées viennent d'elles-mêmes ?
VI. Lorsque vous êtes en difficultés et le secours est plus que nécessaire, En quelles langues criez-vous pour le secours ?
VII. En quelles langues adressez-vous à votre partenaire pour exprimer vos intimités ?

X. Quelles la (les) langue(s) de vos émissions télévisées ou films préférés ?
XI. En quelles langue (s) rédigez-vous avec beaucoup plus de confiance sans avoir peur de commettre des erreurs d'orthographes ?
XII. Quelle(s) est/sont la/les langues des ouvrages ou livres que vous lisez avec passion ?
XIII. Lors des examens ou interrogations, en quelle(s) langue(s) réfléchissez- vous le plus souvent et qui vous aident à trouver aisément les réponses aux questions posées ?

XIV. En quelle(s) langue(s) vos camarades vous expliquent le cours en dehors de l'auditoire ?

XV. En quelle(s) langue(s) préférez-vous que votre pasteur vous prêche à l'église ?

XVI. Quelle(s) langue(s) proposerez- vous qu'on puisse utiliser dans l'enseignement des cours d'anglais pour vous permettre de bien comprendre la matière ?

XVII. Veuillez commenter sur l'utilisation des autres langues dans l'enseignement de la langue anglaise……………………………………

APPENDIX C

TEST ON DIRECT AND INDIRECT SPEECH SUBMITTED TO THE LEARNERS

Student code:……………………

Put the following sentences into indirect speech. Helen said: 'I was busy yesterday'

Bob asked: 'Where did you see the movie?' Tom says: 'Thanks.'

Mum said: 'Hello! How are you?' Bob says:'Wow!'

II. **In which context the tense of the message of the direct speech does not change even if the reporting verb is in the simple past tense? Give an example.**

III. **Put the sentences below into direct speech** He wanted to know if she was married.

The teacher instructed us not to use the simple past tense. They told us that they had not seen them.

She said she would arrive in two days' time.

He answered them that his wife had travelled a week ago.

IV. **Make up two sentences of direct speech (a,b) and put them into indirect one(c,d)**

……………………………………………………………………...

....

....

....

…….. **Referring to question n° IV, mention the changes noticed in (c) and (d)**

....

....

....

SAMPLES

SOME HARD COPIES IN MONOLINGUAL TEST (MALES STUDENTS)

STUDENTS' HARD COPIES OF MONOLINGUAL TEST (FEMALE STUDENTS) STUDENTS' HARD COPIES OF MULTILINGUAL TEST (MALE STUDENTS) HARD COPIES OF MULTILINGUAL TEST (FEMALE STUDENTS)

www.ingramcontent.com/pod-product-compliance
Lightning Source LLC
Chambersburg PA
CBHW061442300426
44114CB00014B/1802